Contents

a note from the author

When I decided to set up Studio, a recruitment company specializing in the interior design sector, it was in the middle of the recession in 2009 and I was twenty-five. I could sense quite a few people thought I was mad. I've always loved a challenge, and at the time I was consumed with the idea of running my own business and being part of the design industry, and I couldn't think of anything else I would rather do.

In the first week I had a client who put faith in Studio and my first freelance placement, Bodrul, a senior retail interior designer at HMKM, was made.

At the back of my mind was the fact that most start-ups fail within the first three years. Looking back, the first three years were certainly the most challenging. At one point I had no fixed abode due to a relationship break-up and all my money had gone into the business.

In my second year, I was evicted from my lovely London office as higher-paying tenants wanted my space. However, the facilities team of the building came to the rescue and offered me the store cupboard for £20 a month, and I snapped their hand off! The cheapest central London office that ever was, well, until the building had an inspection two years on and the fact I had an office set up in there was rumbled – even with a clever Christmas tree and spare furniture disguise! I remember how I used to sneak into the cupboard with my cup of tea and toast when no one was watching and casually stroll out when I thought the coast was clear. But despite my 'surroundings' I was at my computer first thing in the morning and absolutely loved my job, and still do, because one thing I do know is what you put in you get out.

When I left college in 2002, I had no idea where to turn to, how to find a job opportunity, or which companies to apply for. I'll never forget that feeling of being lost and panicked by the next step.

After ten years in business and fifteen years in total recruiting for the interior design industry, I want to give something back. This book is for graduate and experienced interior designers who feel overwhelmed by the next step in their career, and hopefully it will give you all the resources you need to move forward.

I've had some incredible opportunities over the last decade that range from being a judge for six years running for the Design Week Rising Star Award, host and compere for the renowned Restaurant & Bar Design Awards, and being a regular columnist for *Interior Designer* magazine.

Studio only exists because incredibly talented designers and design consultancies put their faith in me, and for that I'm eternally grateful. Thank you.

Interior designers continue to inspire me with their talent every day, and it is a joy and a privilege to be part of such a diverse and creative industry.

Hopefully this book will be a reference throughout your exciting career ahead. Enjoy!

Lucy Painter
Founder, Studio

Chapter 1:

the underdog

Not all CVs are created equal.

When I put an advert out for a junior interior designer, I will receive, on average, 130 applications.

But from this selection, only five to eight designers are introduced to the company.

This was one of the driving factors for writing this book. I want all 130 junior interior designers to have an opportunity to be put forward for the job.

What makes an application stand out from the crowd? It is often in the detail: a CV and portfolio that are clearly and beautifully presented and where the content of both has been thought through.

CVs are often the underdog to the portfolio, but it is just as important to spend as much time refining your CV as you do with your portfolio of work. A blank piece of paper is the start of an opportunity, not something to be dreaded.

Writing a CV can be quite laborious, and sometimes you don't even know where to start. My advice would be to write down all of your achievements, strengths, personal qualities, and projects you've worked on.

Having viewed thousands of CVs, here are six elements you should definitely include at any stage of your career:

- Profile
- Key skills
- Education
- Computer skills
- Software knowledge
- Employment history
- Projects experience

Over the next few pages, I will go into these in more detail.

The CVs that stand out to me are the ones that are uncluttered, where attention has been paid to spelling, grammar, and content, and above all that are a reflection of the applicant's personality. Imagine seeing a CV where the text is scrunched together in small columns and is eight pages long ... I see these more often than you'd think and it's really not attractive – especially in a professional setting where everything is about presentation.

CV dos and don'ts

When you start to write your CV, keep the following in mind:

- *If a potential employer only looked at your CV, would they be just as impressed as if they only saw your portfolio?*

- *Your CV is an example of your writing ability; it gives an insight into your personality and the care you take putting a document together.*

- *As your experience and project exposure progresses, your CV starts to allow you to add information about projects that may not be in the sample portfolio you send out.*

Photos

If you are trying to decide whether a selfie is suitable for your CV, then the answer is NO! Keep it for your social media, as I guarantee you will be searched for online before you're called in for an interview anyway.

Project examples

A few key photos of previous projects or a sketch is absolutely fine if you want to entice your future employer, but don't overload your CV as that is what your portfolio is for.

File type

PDF is by far the preferred file type for an applicant's CV and portfolio, simply because it's easy to view, its refined and it's compatible with everything. Feel free to have a web link to a fuller portfolio of work, but always send a sample PDF with your application.

File size

You don't want your CV and portfolio to go into a spam folder. Avoid this by keeping both to a combined maximum file size of 15 Mb.

Not in the neighbourhood?

Take your address off your CV if you currently live a long way from the company you are applying to. Employers may feel guilty about inviting you in for an interview or assume you may have to find accommodation before you can accept a job. It is not worth the risk missing out on an interview.

Mobile friendly

Decision-makers have demanding jobs and will review their emails when they are travelling or waiting for a meeting. This means that most directors will review your CV and portfolio on their phone. So before you send out your CV and portfolio, make sure you view it on your phone to see how it clear it is.

Web links to portfolios can be risky. If the link to your website doesn't open seamlessly, your application will be deleted. That's why it is so important to have a sample portfolio of work in a PDF format to accompany your CV. If you are including a web link, don't hide it in a bulky section of text. Make it easy to find.

9

the profile section

Who are you?

Think of the profile section of your CV as an introduction to you: a summary of who you are and what you're looking for. Many people find this section tricky to put together, but it's worth spending the time to get it right, particularly if you're applying for a position that's a step up – or a big change – from your current one.

Your profile should be unique to you, and there is no single correct way to go about it. Here are a few general points to keep in mind.

Writing style

Candidates are sometimes tempted to pack this section with fancy words that they wouldn't normally use in order to sound formal. This can make it hard to read:

'A tenacious, loquacious, scrupulous designer, I am extraordinarily proud of my ability to produce creative, innovative, forward-thinking, and pioneering designs that boast both commercial viability and aesthetic significance.'

But don't over-simplify either:

'I am a designer. I work hard and I do good designs. I have done lots of different design projects.'

These examples may be extreme, but it's easy to go a little too far to one end of the spectrum while trying to get away from the other! To strike a balance between variety and readability, challenge yourself not to start more than a couple of sentences with 'I'. Once you've written your first draft, try reading it out loud to someone else. If it doesn't sound natural, or they can't quickly make sense of what you're trying to say, it might be worth simplifying your language.

Here's a better example:

'As a hard-working design professional with three years' experience in the industry, I pride myself on my ability to produce designs that are both creative and commercially sound.'

Targeting

One of the most common suggestions that I give people who ask for CV feedback is 'You could make it a little clearer what you're looking for.' The profile is a great place to start solving this problem and, if you're applying for a few different kinds of roles, tailor it to each role. If you're sending it speculatively to a recruitment agent, this will also allow you to set out exactly what kind of role you'd like them to put you forward for.

For example, if you are a junior interior designer looking for a job in a company specializing in retail design but have yet to gain any retail project experience, you might write something like:

'Over the last year I have been working at [company] as a junior interior designer, where I have worked on client presentations, researching source materials, and curating mood boards. The role requires regularly liaising with suppliers and contractors, and designing layouts in Vectorworks. I have a passion for retail interiors and would love the opportunity to develop my skills within your design studio.'

If you're applying for a few different kinds of roles, tailor it to each role.

showcasing key skills

What can you do?

I would advise at any level that you include a list of your skills at the beginning of your CV. This will help to highlight your suitability for a role and catch the eye of a scan-reader. These skills will develop over time, depending on how your level of experience grows.

Some designers prefer to keep the skills section quite brief, but here I've included a fuller combination for each level, which may spark some inspiration! The following are examples of keys skills you would tend to find on a CV from a graduate through to associate/director level. Across all levels there is an assumption that the company you are applying to will know what you are capable of as they can see your job title.

For junior roles especially, companies will receive, on average, over a hundred CVs for one position. Being clear about your skills helps them understand your ability at a glance; if you tick most of the boxes, they are more likely to invite you in for an interview.

Being clear about your skills helps them understand your ability at a glance.

Graduate

Writing a CV after graduation can be hard as you may struggle to articulate your skills and experience. Don't underestimate yourself! Doing a degree engages a huge range of skills, including research, communication, concept skills, technical ability, teamwork, experience in delivering presentations, and organization, to name a few! Talking about your key skills in more depth when you are a junior will give your CV more depth and set a good impression to potential employers, as per this example. You can keep the skill set section to more of a bullet point format, but make sure your CV doesn't look too sparse.

- *Communication*

  The ability to articulate verbally in a fluent and professional manner

  Confident at explaining design ideas through regular presentations

  Written communication skills when creating feasibility studies and design briefs

- *Digital*

  Confident ability in using Vectorworks. Working on plans, sections, and elevations

  Proficient in using Adobe Creative Suite

  Flexible to work on either PC or Mac

- *Organization*

  Managing to complete several projects at once throughout heavily coursework-based subjects and meeting all deadlines

- *Creativity*

  Passion for trends and influences from all aspects of life. I have a creative mind full of innovative and interesting ideas

  Initial ideas and inspirations for projects often emerge from sketches that can be seen throughout my portfolio

- *Commercial awareness*

  Keeping up to date with the design world and current inspirations by reading collections of design journals, while also searching Twitter and Pinterest

  This year I have attended a number of design events, including 100% Design and Clerkenwell Design Week

Junior designer

Once you have gained industry experience, your skills will have developed hugely. It is imperative you are clear about what you have been involved with as it can vary greatly from company to company.

Here are some examples of key skills you are likely to see on a junior's CV:

- *Researching for projects and creating mood boards*
- *Create and maintain new materials and FF&E library, resourcing suppliers and manufacturers*
- *Technical drawings: space planning, lighting plans, sections, elevations*
- *Rendering drawings in Photoshop*
- *Creating 3D visuals*
- *Site surveys*
- *Assisting in preparing presentations for clients*

Middleweight interior designer

This is a very exciting time in your career. You are confident in your ability and have developed and refined your skills. You will know what your strengths and weaker areas are, what projects you have enjoyed working on, and what direction you would like your career to take.

There will inevitably be areas which you would like more experience in or areas you want to develop, for example, attending site more often, the opportunity to present to clients, or finding a company that will give you more independence on projects. You may be very good at technical drawings and visualizing, which in turn means you haven't had much exposure working on the initial concept stage of a project, presenting work, or seeing projects on site.

Don't panic; I hear this frequently. Just make sure in your next role, whether that is in the same company or at a new studio, you ensure you are clear that you want to gain more exposure in all areas of the design process.

Here are some examples of key skills you are likely to see on a middleweight's CV:

- *Concept design: interpreting the client's brief, working on initial concept stages of a project*
- *Strong freehand sketching and visualizing skills*
- *Experience at presenting work to clients*
- *Technical drawings: working on full technical drawing packages*
- *Liaising with suppliers and contractors*
- *Sourcing FF&E*
- *Creating and maintaining client relationships*
- *Attend site with a director and overseeing a project from concept through to completion*

Senior interior designer

Officially the 'all-round designer'! You will have been involved in working on all aspects of a project independently, from concept through to completion, only checking in with directors at key points of a project.

Employers will expect you to be able to communicate your ideas confidently to clients and the design team, and have extensive site experience and confident negotiating skills. Depending on the size of a company and its team structure, it is highly likely you will be managing a small team of middleweight and junior designers.

Here are some examples of key skills you are likely to see on a senior's CV:

- *Working on projects from concept through to completion*
- *Strong freehand sketching ability*
- *Ability to manage a small design team*
- *Respond creatively to business briefs and expectations*
- *Confident in presenting to new and existing clients*
- *Ensure projects are delivered on time and within budget*
- *Manage and deliver approvals: landlords, building control, planning, etc.*
- *Keeping up to date with current trends and insights*

Team leader/associate/ design director/ head of interiors

The roles after senior designer can vary hugely across companies, hence why there are so many job titles listed above. While not all roles will be the same, one thing is for sure: companies will be looking for you to take on more of a strategic overview of the business and contribute your ideas and thoughts to the company's ethos and direction.

The skills needed for an associate tend to be focused around your ability to lead teams, juggle multiple workloads, and having the business acumen to identify new leads and opportunities. You will be asked to offer insight, analysis, and opinions about a broad range of topics.

Here are some examples of key skills you are likely to see on an associate's CV:

- *Lead creative pitches and client presentations*
- *Team management: delegating tasks, understanding strengths and weaknesses of a team, and mentoring talent*
- *Creative vision: identifying opportunities and challenges for clients*
- *Responsibility for overall project delivery: initial briefing, writing proposals, project organization, budgets, presentations, and overseeing quality of work*
- *Nurturing client relationships and generating new business*
- *Contribute to development of the company structure, values, and culture*
- *Recruitment requirements, managing resources, and conducting interviews for freelance and permanent staff*

15

Education

―――

This is a key element to your CV especially if you have a degree. If a degree is your highest level of education, then this is generally all that is required on your CV. As a junior designer, you may want to mention your dissertation project. This can often be a good talking point at an interview.

Some designers like to list their A level and GCSE results. I would advise against listing all of your GCSEs individually and just summarize your grades. For example:

―――

BA (Hons) Interior Design (2:1) – 2016–2019 Nottingham Trent University

3 A levels: Art (A), Design (A*) and Psychology (B) – 2011–2016

Software

―――

Always list the computer programs you are confident working on near the top of your CV. Naturally you will be fluent in some programs more than others. Avoid adding software on your CV that you don't feel comfortable working with or wouldn't want to retrain in. It will waste a lot of time for both parties, especially unwanted calls from recruiters about jobs with companies who use that software! Rather than writing a list, some designers like to demonstrate their level of skills for each software, for example:

Skills
―

Adobe Photoshop	● ● ● ● ●	Revit	● ● ● ● ○
Adobe InDesign	● ● ● ● ○	SketchUp	● ● ● ● ●
Adobe Illustrator	● ● ● ● ○	V-Ray	● ● ● ● ○
AutoCAD	● ● ● ● ●	Microsoft Office	● ● ● ● ○
Vectorworks	● ● ● ● ●	Merlin Project	● ● ● ● ○

SOFTWARE SKILLS:

Avoid adding software on your CV that you don't feel comfortable working with.

Project and work experience

Exposure

Projects are your golden nuggets! It is absolutely essential you list the projects you have worked on and let them shine through. Many times, I have seen projects hidden among masses of text and not given the attention they deserve. As a general rule, list the projects you have worked on after each employment. This is also a great way of mentioning projects you have worked on that may not necessarily be in your portfolio.

Try and include as much project information as you can. This should comprise of the type of project and your involvement. If you know more information about the size and value of the project, include this as well. Imagine the company did not have access to your portfolio when you write your list. Here are a few examples of how to list your project experience:

Penthouse apartment, Central London
Complete refurbishment

I worked alongside a senior designer on the concept designs and presentations, space planning, technical detailing, and FF&E specification.

Five-star hotel, France
Listed building

£10 million refit of the restaurant, bar, and bedrooms. I was involved in the team, working on the initial concept phases of the project, creating mood boards and visuals, specifying materials and furniture, and producing technical drawings.

Costa Coffee
Roll-out of twelve coffee shops across the UK

Working on the technical drawing package and following the brand guidelines.

One Hyde Park
Developed the FF&E scheme design for the common areas, reception, and spa

Nike
Pitch presentation for a pop-up stand in Shoreditch, working alongside a senior interior designer

Lululemon Athletica
Flagship store, Regent Street, London

Working with the creative lead on the initial concept and strategy for the store. I developed the concept design, worked on the presentations, created visuals in Cinema 4D, and delivered the technical drawing pack in Vectorworks for freelance and permanent staff.

Chapter 2:

the
main event

Showcasing you and your
portfolio in the best possible light.

making your portfolio shine

Portfolios are a demonstration of your skills and examples of projects you have worked on. As a junior interior designer, ensure you present your work beautifully and that it clearly demonstrates your key skills. Throughout your career your portfolio will need continually updating, as new projects will need to be added and older projects taken out or swapped with better work samples. Here are a few top tips.

Explain projects

Include a short summary for each project you are showcasing. If there is work in your portfolio that you have worked on as part of a team, clearly state exactly which elements you worked on, e.g. the concept visuals and furniture selection.

Be relevant

Order projects according to the company you are meeting. Employers like the work that is most relevant to theirs. So if they work on residential interiors, put your residential work first.

Additional documents

Some candidates have a separate technical portfolio attachment where they include a drawing pack or a collection of technical drawings. This frees up more creative space in your main portfolio.

Strengths

Inevitably, over your career you will find that your strengths start to shine through in your portfolio. For example, if your freehand sketching is very strong, it is likely most companies will utilize you to work on pitches and the concept stages of projects, and your portfolio will clearly demonstrate this.

Creative skills

It is fairly common for designers to show work they have completed in their own time, such as photography or graphic design, towards the end of their portfolio. I've known directors to really pick up on these elements. For example, one candidate had completed a pop-up stand for a festival with some friends. This caught the attention of the director and, as a consequence, they invited her in for an interview.

Digital or traditional?

As long as you can clearly see the work and it is well presented, displaying it on a tablet/laptop or in a printed format is fine. Many designers now do a mixture of both: they will present their portfolio on a laptop or tablet at the interview but will also bring along their sketchbook and a printed drawing pack to support it.

Low battery/no Wi-Fi

It's basic stuff, but if you are only showcasing your portfolio on a laptop, make sure you have enough battery on your computer and that the portfolio doesn't rely on the internet. If there are two or three separate files, ensure they are easily accessible in the same folder.

Basic errors

A scruffy portfolio, which hasn't been given much attention, will instantly put off future employers. I've witnessed talented designers be rejected for jobs based on the fact their portfolio wasn't well presented, it had been thrown together at the last minute, or the projects were not in order.

How many times have I seen 'designer' or 'interiors' spelled incorrectly? Too many! Spellcheck the wording on your portfolio. As portfolios are often created in programs that do not have a spellcheck function, it can be very easy to miss a typo. Don't be that 'desiger'.

21

Many designers present on a mixture of a <u>tablet/laptop</u> and <u>a printed format.</u>

concept design

It is important to show how your concept ideas relate to the initial brief, which then guides you through the design process. The concept stage of the project can be demonstrated through sketches, visuals, and mood boards. You will be asked at interview to talk through your thought process on each project, hence why it's an integral part of the portfolio.

22

- *Sketches (freehand drawing ability): don't throw away your sketches! Even if they are little doodles of a furniture detail, keep them! The easiest way is to keep a sketchbook. Employers love to see how you work out ideas. They are not looking for refined work, just an example of how you think things through.*

- *Visuals: created using 3D software, such as Cinema 4D, SketchUp, 3ds Max, etc.*

- *Mood boards: if they are material boards, a photo is fine. Or if it was an online collage, then a copy of this will suffice.*

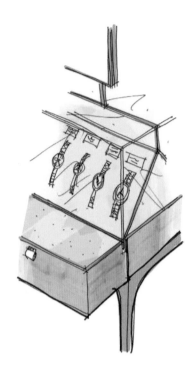

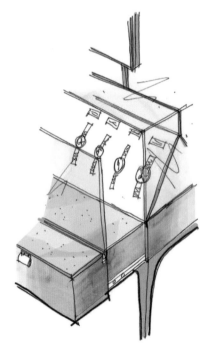

*When presenting work to clients, showing a sketch next to a pictures of sample
furniture allows them to visualize the look and feel more easily.*

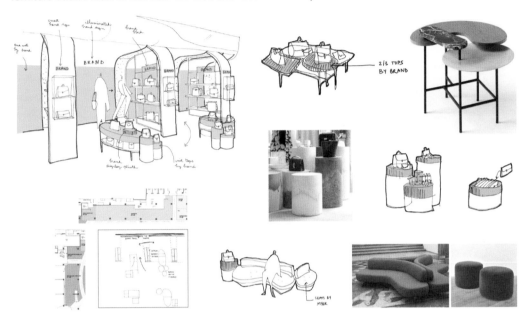

*This is an example of the progression of concept ideas from very loose sketches,
which progress to more refined 3D SketchUp visuals and finally into Cinema 4D.*

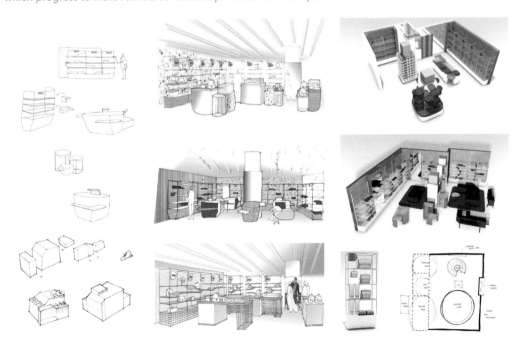

Above:
*Concept sketches for a flagship store, Australia and the UK
Virgile + Partners*

24

Above:
Concept sketches for Shopper Stop department store, Gargaon, Mumbai
Dalziel & Pow

Sketches courtesy of:

Héloïse Motte

Héloïse studied Applied Arts and Interior Design in Paris and then did a master's degree in Interior Architecture, Product Design and Graphic Design Strategy. After graduating, Héloïse made her way to London to gain experience in the fast-paced aspects of retail and joined gpstudio, where she worked on projects such as Theo Fennell, Fortnum & Mason, John Lewis, and multiple Jigsaw stores. Héloïse then moved to HMKM and was exposed to larger retail projects, such as the Primark flagship in Amsterdam and the Tryano department store in Abu Dhabi.

With a passion for illustration, Héloïse now takes on private commissions while working on hospitality and retail interiors at Virgile + Partners as a freelance senior interior designer. Recent projects include the refurbishment of Harrods, TSUM in Russia, and the Intercontinental in Germany.

Becky Simpson

Becky graduated in 2010 with a degree in Interior Architecture. After her first job working on a cruise ship project as an AutoCAD assistant, Becky moved to Imagination where she worked on many strategic design pitches for various retail brands, as well working with The Body Shop. Her next permanent role was with Campaign as a middleweight interior designer, designing experiential retail interiors for Selfridges. Becky soon progressed to a senior interior designer, in a new role at Household and created prestigious, award-winning projects for Christian Louboutin and The White Company.

At the end of 2017 Becky decided to take the leap into the world of freelancing and continues to work with some of London's most prestigious design consultancies as a lead concept designer.

25

technical drawings

While they're not the most glamorous, technical drawings are an essential part of any portfolio to demonstrate your knowledge. It is important to put snapshots of your technical drawing capability and ensure you include:

- *Plans: space planning, lighting plans, etc.*
- *Elevations and sections: external elevations, internal sections*
- *Joinery details: this may be of furniture, partitions, etc.*
- *Fixture and fitting details*

26

Recommended reading

Design Drawing by Francis D. K. Ching is a classic book on the basic principles around illustrating technical drawings.

Jess Codrington & Christopher Boniface

Jess and Christopher set up their own business, Draw Design Studio, in 2016, which specializes in retail and commercial interior design. They originally met twelve years ago working n-house for high-street fashion retailer River Island where they designed architectural interiors. Here you'll find their top tips for taking on technical drawings like a pro.

Think about who you're trying to communicate your drawings to – a graphic, colourful approach can help support conceptual ideas for pitches to clients, whereas more technical information might be more suitable for contractors. The skill of technical communication is an art. Layout, scale, and consistency in style make a huge difference to someone looking at the information you're trying to get across. Even with industry standards you can create a communication style unique to you.

Key tips for technical drawings:

- *Have a look through some of your old projects and ask yourself the following: could you improve on your technical communication? Would revising the layout, use of colour, line weights, or opacities help sell the information more? Are you consistent in your presentational style? Are you keeping clean lines and alignment on your pages?* **See example A (overleaf).**

- *Remember, what you draw will get built! In a more visual world, it's easy to forget the level of detail and information required to make concepts a physical reality. Detail drawing is a craft built from years of experience; detailing clarifies an intent and shows you have a real understanding of how materials work.* **See example B (overleaf).**

- *Call out some specific junction details that could make a difference to how your design is built. Perhaps pick a corner detail or zoom in on where two junctions meet? See example C (overleaf).*

- *If specifying materials or products, do your research. Manufacturers will usually have information on how their materials behave, from how to junction them to the thickness of the material or how it needs to be supported. See example D (overleaf).*

- *Look at the built environment around you and try to draw how that is detailed. We are surrounded by beautiful details and junctions that someone will have had to draw or design. Sketch what you see – how are the corners junctioned? Are there shadow gaps? Is there a bespoke edge detail?*

- *Technical drawings don't have to be CAD-based – freehand sketches can cross-communicate and show you are technically 'bilingual'. And quick sketches can resolve questions in meetings without even speaking. See example E (overleaf).*

- *Add a few sketch details to your portfolio; this will show you are versatile in how you communicate technically.*

- *Use grid paper to help guide your lines. Try to freehand sketch as much as possible; the more you do it, the easier it is.*

27

Technical drawing examples

Example A

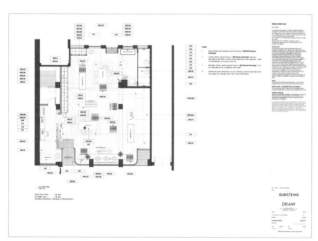

Example B

Example C

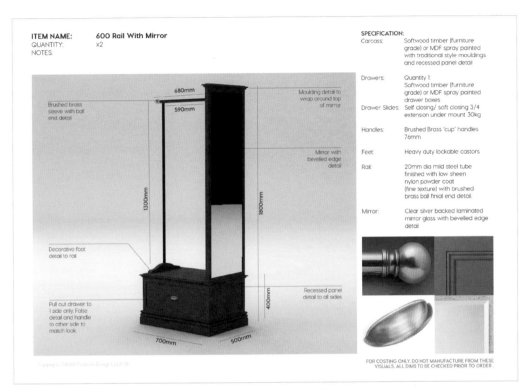

ITEM NAME: 600 Rail With Mirror
QUANTITY: x2
NOTES:

Brushed brass sleeve with ball end detail

Moulding detail to wrap around top of mirror

Mirror with bevelled edge detail

680mm

590mm

1300mm

1800mm

Decorative foot detail to rail

Pull out drawer to 1 side only. False detail and handle to other side to match look.

400mm

Recessed panel detail to all sides

700mm

500mm

SPECIFICATION:

Carcass: Softwood timber (furniture grade) or MDF spray painted with traditional style mouldings and recessed panel detail

Drawers: Quantity 1: Softwood timber (furniture grade) or MDF spray painted drawer boxes

Drawer Slides: Self closing/ soft closing 3/4 extension under mount 30kg

Handles: Brushed Brass 'cup' handles 76mm

Feet: Heavy duty lockable castors

Rail: 20mm dia mild steel tube finished with low sheen nylon powder coat (fine texture) with brushed brass ball finial end detail.

Mirror: Clear silver backed laminated mirror glass with bevelled edge detail

FOR COSTING ONLY. DO NOT MANUFACTURE FROM THESE VISUALS. ALL DIMS TO BE CHECKED PRIOR TO ORDER.

29

Example D

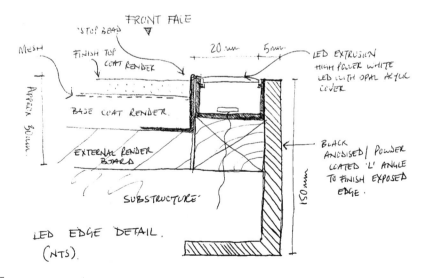

FRONT FACE

'STOP BEAD'

MESH

FINISH TOP COAT RENDER

20 mm   5mm

LED EXTRUSION HIGH POWER WHITE LED WITH OPAL ACRYLIC COVER

APPROX 50mm

BASE COAT RENDER

EXTERNAL RENDER BOARD

BLACK ANODISED/ POWDER COATED 'L' ANGLE TO FINISH EXPOSED EDGE.

150mm

SUBSTRUCTURE

LED EDGE DETAIL.
(NTS).

Example E

finished photos

These may not be available, which is absolutely fine. However, if they are available, add them in.

For portfolio examples from established designers, take a look at the profiles from page 86.

30

Right:
Wedgewood,
Waterford and
Royal Copenhagen
at Harrods, London
Studio Found, 2019

Chapter 3:

finding work

Opportunity can be found in
the most unexpected places.

the four 'angles'

Looking for work is time consuming and requires patience and perseverance. The typical approach is to only apply to job adverts, but by being more tactical and attacking the search from all four angles outlined in the diagram below, you will develop new contacts and leads, and soon enough opportunities will start to find you! The majority of designers I speak to who have been out of work for more than a couple of weeks have only approached looking for a job with two of the four approaches.

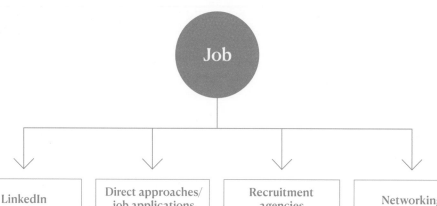

Job

LinkedIn	Direct approaches/ job applications	Recruitment agencies	Networking
Have a presence:	**Finding companies to approach directly from:**	**Working with a specialist recruitment agency to find you work**	**Let your network know that you're actively looking for work. Utilize your network of contacts:**
Keep your profile updated	Press and magazine articles		Colleagues
Comment on industry news	Top 100 ranking charts		Friends
Post ideas or previous work	Interior design directory (see page 190)		Clients
Write articles	Companies shortlisted for awards		Contractors and suppliers
Apply to LinkedIn jobs			Recruiters
Connect with all contacts – 'Triad of connections' (see page 42)	**Submitting your CV and portfolio to job adverts via industry job boards**		

1. LinkedIn

This is a fantastic platform for you to find contacts, but more importantly it allows people who are recruiting to find you. More and more agencies are utilizing LinkedIn to approach designers directly and save on paying recruitment agency fees.

This platform is designed for you to connect with contacts you may not have met in person, so send out requests to connect to people you would like to be part of your network. But remember, the design industry is fiercely competitive, and out of site is out of mind. Therefore, it is imperative your profile is up to date.

- *Writing the 'About' section on LinkedIn can be the same or similar to the one you have written for your CV profile. It is a place for you to sell your skills, give a brief overview of your experience, and mention projects you have been involved in.*

- *Under each area of work experience, keep it succinct and add details of key projects you have been involved in.*

- *There is a facility where you can add an attachment to your profile so people can view your portfolio of work.*

- *I often find designers' contact information is out of date on LinkedIn, which may be to do with people's personal privacy settings, but if you do add your email address, it will allow companies who do not have LinkedIn Premium to contact you. Otherwise, it means they are unable to approach you unless you are*

connected. By the time you have accepted their LinkedIn request, they may already be in conversation with someone else. If you are worried about spam, then set up a separate email address purely for LinkedIn.

- *Recruiters will often use key words to search for candidates. For example, if you can use AutoCAD and specialize in residential interiors, then ensure 'AutoCAD', 'residential', and 'interiors' are included in the key skills area.*

- *Ensure your profile photo is the best reflection of you. Ask a close friend for their opinion if you are unsure. Remember LinkedIn is for building your business community and job searching. It's not a dating site or Facebook.*

- *Make sure you are receiving alerts and turn your notifications on.*

LinkedIn is a great tool to find contacts within companies that you want to approach with your CV and portfolio. If you follow companies you like, then you will be updated with their jobs when they are recruiting.

Social media privacy settings

Companies will often search you on social media before they invite you in for an interview. Check your privacy settings on any sites you want to keep personal, and be vigilant in what you post as it can be interpreted incorrectly. I know a designer who had commented on an article not related to the industry, but the company perceived it in the wrong way and cancelled the interview.

Friends and former colleagues

Each of these people you know also has a wide network. Keep them updated if you are looking for work. Ask for any referrals or recommendations on possible opportunities they hear about. When going to events, invite friends and colleagues to go with you.

There is a really good episode of *HBR IdeaCast* by David Burkus called 'Networking Myths Dispelled' that is worth checking out.

35

2. Direct approaches/job applications

Cover letters in the design sector are a thing of the past and are rarely read. A concise email will work perfectly in its absence. Keep your introductory email to 500 words and include the following key points employers are looking for:

- *What level you are as a designer*
- *Availability/notice period*
- *Software skills*
- *Projects you have had experience working on*
- *When you would be free to interview*

To catch their attention, mention a project of theirs you admire or congratulate them for a recent award they may have won. Or, to be very different, send a copy of your CV and portfolio in the post as well! As always, ensure your CV and portfolio are updated and your portfolio is tailored to the company's projects.

Following up with a call may or may not help, but I personally don't think it does any harm. Use the call to check they have received your application and find out when you should expect to hear back from them. Make a note of whom you have spoken to. Send a connect request to the directors and studio managers on LinkedIn.

Be very careful if you copy and paste email introductions. On a number of occasions, I have received an email addressed to someone else, mentions a company the applicant had emailed previously, or is irrelevant to the job they are applying to. It is not a good first impression!

Be very careful if you <u>copy and paste</u> email introductions – I have received emails addressed to someone else!

3. Recruitment agencies

When you look for a recruitment company to work with, find a company that specializes in interior design. Design consultancies, as a rule, will try and recruit junior interior designers directly rather than pay a recruitment fee. When a recruitment agency is given a permanent vacancy, the employer is paying a fee, so they will expect to be sent candidates who match the brief by at least 90%. Do not be offended if you are rejected for jobs you have applied for and that you think you are perfect for. Here are some other key things to consider when approaching recruiters.

Knowledge is power

Make sure you utilize a recruitment agency for their knowledge. Gain feedback on your CV and portfolio, find out what the market is like, ask if they can supply you with a list of companies to apply to directly, and let them know you are keen to be informed of future opportunities.

Arrange a meet-up

Once you have sent your CV and portfolio to a recruiter, arrange a time with them to talk through your work to see if they can help you look for any jobs. Larger recruitment agents often have separate consultants for permanent and contract roles, so make sure you're in touch with someone whose specialism suits your needs.

A brief brief

When you give the recruiter a brief of what you are looking for, try and keep the key criteria for a new job to a maximum of three points. I have had candidates who have been very specific in what they are looking for, which is absolutely fine, but sometimes I'm reluctant to run jobs by them in case it isn't exactly what they are looking for. It is better for recruiters to run more jobs by you than none at all. You don't have to be put forward for the jobs, but it will give you an idea of who is recruiting and the type of companies that particular recruiters work with.

Your details, your rules

If you don't want recruiters to send your CV and portfolio out without your permission, make sure they're aware of this. This may sound like common sense but, believe me, I know designers who have had their details sent out without their permission. If the recruiter says that they are 'unable to tell you who the client is', do not take this as an excuse as due to GDPR regulations they are your personal details and you have a right to know where they're going.

Stay in touch

Check in with the recruiter on a regular basis either via phone, text, or email especially if you haven't heard from them. When an interview is arranged for you, if you are unsure of anything, call the recruiter to go over the details of the job and the company to check you haven't missed anything.

37

4. Networking

When I set up Studio, I spent the first three months out of the office meeting companies and designers. This resulted in referrals, new opportunities, and the foundations of long-term business relations. It is absolutely vital to be seen at these events, as when potential employers have an opportunity, you will be the person who comes to mind first.

Get some face time

Relationships are not built on email. Events, talks, and exhibitions are fantastic opportunities to meet with new contacts in the design industry face-to-face, build on existing relationships, and absorb lots of new influences and ideas. The great thing about the design industry is there are lots of events hosted throughout the year. Make a note of what's going on in your diary so you don't miss out.

Suppliers are a great way to get into these events as often they have tickets to events for designers. You will find suppliers deal with lots of different people and practices. This equates to lots of new introductions and potential leads for new jobs.

Talk the talk and then follow-up

If you want to build connections at events, business cards are essential. It is much easier to exchange a business card than risk the embarrassment of not remembering the person's name while you mess around entering their details into your phone. Make sure you follow-up with people after the event, especially if they're willing to offer business advice or know of any job openings.

Many business leaders now present talks or are part of panels at these events, offering insight and helping you build on your knowledge. Hang around after talks to network with the speakers and other attendees. They are good leading points for any introduction emails. Mention you found their talk intuitive or spoke to them after the event. This will go down very well!

Relationships are not built on email – get some face time.

In the know

Below are a list of publications, awards, and events to help you stay up to date on companies, projects and trends, and use for inspiration. The British Institute of Interior Design (BIID) **biid.co.uk** is a great source of information to find out about exhibitions, trade shows and networking events in the industry.

Magazine publications online/offline	Industry awards	Industry events
FX	Restaurant & Bar Design Awards	100% Design
Elle Decoration	FX Awards	Clerkenwell Design Week
*Wallpaper**	Design Week Awards	Tent
Hospitality Interiors	Creative Retail Awards	Milan
Dezeen	World Interior News Awards	Retail Expo
Design Week	House & Garden Top 100 Awards	Sleeper
Interior Designer	SBID Awards	Restaurant & Bar Design Show
Interior Design		London Design Festival
World Interiors News		
FRAME		

Your contacts: organized

Keep a record of your contacts on an Excel spreadsheet. It will become invaluable over time. A simple spreadsheet will allow you to keep track on who you have contacted, where and when, jobs you have applied for, and people you have met at events. A simple template like this works well:

Name	Position/company	Email	Date/notes
Lucy Painter	Director, Studio	lucy@studio.eu.com	9/2019 – sent my CV and portfolio for review

Triad of connections

We often only think about the people we liaise with on a day-to-day basis. The exercise below is a good way to clearly see who you are connected to. Use this exercise to confirm how extended your network really is. In the coloured circles below, list all the people you know. Include family, friends, work colleagues, and acquaintances. For example, a colleague you sit next to each day (red), a client you liaise with regularly for an ongoing project at work (green), and the director of a lighting company you have met twice at site meetings (blue).

When connecting on LinkedIn, reach out to all of your reds, greens, and blues. If you are looking for advice on your portfolio or CV, try reaching out to the people in the green and blue circles. These contacts are further enough removed to give you constructive feedback and will offer a different perspective to the people closest to you.

40

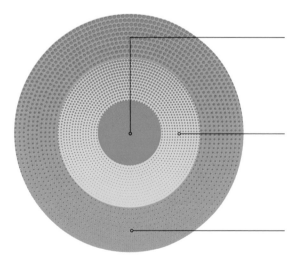

Red connections

People you know very well and see on a regular basis.

Green connections

Most coworkers, local community, acquaintances, and other people you interact with on a frequent basis (but are not your friends).

Blue connections

Have never met on a one-to-one basis. People with whom you do transactions or sat in a meeting with once before.

Your career can take many paths

It isn't uncommon for your strengths to lead you into a specialism. For example, if you enjoy using Cinema 4D and produce visuals quickly, you may move into a visualizer role and progress to leading a visualizing team within a studio. Check out some other career paths below.

Skill set:

FF&E focused	Strong sketching/ concept skills	Good technical ability	Good visualizing skills	Project co-ordination /management	All-rounder

... could lead to a career as a ...

Junior FF&E designer	Concept designer	Interior technician	3D visualizer	Design manager	Junior
Middleweight FF&E designer	Pitch designer	Senior technician	Senior 3D visualizer	Senior design manager	Middleweight
Senior FF&E designer	Lead creative	Technical lead	Head of visualizing	Head of design management	Senior
Head of FF&E					Team leader
					Associate director

... or even running your own business

Chapter 4:

interview preparation

Simple checklists to get you interview-ready.

'By failing to prepare, you are preparing to fail.'

44

– Benjamin Franklin

Although, on the whole, design interviews are fairly relaxed, it doesn't mean you should be. Preparation is absolutely key; nerves can take hold of the situation, and you will find your preparation will kick in. Running through the following questions and key points in advance of your interview will inevitably help you engage with any questions that are put to you. It goes without saying that you should aim to arrive at your interview five minutes before the agreed time. Make sure you have the address to hand, your route is planned, and you have the company's phone number available to call if you become delayed.

What do you know about the company?

Have a look on their website and, if you can, visit any of their projects. Form an opinion that you can discuss in the interview. Take note of any awards they may have received or have been shortlisted for. What do you think of projects in their portfolio of work?

Why do you want to move from your current role and why are you interested in this company specifically?

What skills are you hoping to develop in your next role? what do you want to learn from this company? And what project experience are you looking for? Go through the job description and make sure you talk through your strengths that match the job description and any relevant experiences.

Explain your current/ previous job role

Set the scene: who was in your team? What was the company structure? What were your responsibilities? What projects were/are you working on and what skills have you developed while working there? Keep your answers positive when talking about a previous company as it doesn't bode well hearing negative comments.

Talking through your projects

Explain the brief from the client. Where did the concept come from and how was it executed? Talk through any challenges you had to overcome — that may be anything from budget restrictions, working on listed buildings, planning problems, and time constraints.

Discuss challenges with previous clients

They are asking you this as it allows you to discuss how you would deal with difficult situations; it demonstrates your communications skills, how you solved a problem, who you had to liaise with to rectify it, and the processes you went through.

Current trends and influences

Where do you find your inspiration for projects? What trends/projects/ designers' work have you admired recently and why? Discuss the strategy and insight behind your projects.

→

What has been your biggest achievement in the last few years?

This question may not come up in an interview, but do think about what you have achieved in your personal and professional life; if it's relevant, talk about it and be proud!

Mentoring/ managing designers

Give examples of how you have utilized your team's strengths, and when you gave them responsibility or offered guidance. Discuss difficult scenarios you have faced and how you have overcome these/ how you sought guidance.

Strengths and areas of development

It is inevitable you will have strengths in some areas and less exposure to other elements of a job. This is absolutely fine. Remember to discuss this in a positive way. Try and show a balanced portfolio, incorporating sketches, concept work, visuals, technical drawings, and finished photos from various projects. You may not have all aspects of every project and that is fine.

Ambitions

Don't be afraid to tell your future employer your ambitions and goals for the long or short term. It shows enthusiasm and passion for the industry. Discuss what you have achieved to date, be that taking a certain project from concept to completion, developing skills in a new software, or having the opportunity to work with a client or project you had on your bucket list.

What motivates you?

This may not be asked directly; however, it's good to think about what it is that motivates you in work and life to get you into a positive frame of mind before the interview.

46

Take a few minutes to refresh your memory on previous projects.

Revisit your portfolio

It is easy to forget a project when it was a few years ago. Take a few minutes to refresh your memory on previous projects. Order the work samples to show the most relevant projects first. If you have a lot of work, pick two or three key projects to focus on. Going through your portfolio shouldn't take longer than 20 minutes.

Notes

Take a notebook into the interview to have questions or key points you want to discuss easily accessible. This is especially useful if you draw a blank or want to make a note of anything that comes up.

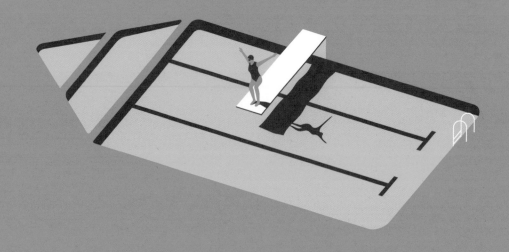

Chapter 5:

freelancing

Taking the plunge by going it alone.

Having recruited freelancers for design companies for over fifteen years, I know there are a number of elements you may want to consider before you take the leap into the freelancing world. Freelancing is a fantastic way to meet other designers, see how different design companies work, experience a variety of projects, and on the whole earn good money and schedule time off when you want. It can also be very quiet for long, unexpected periods of time. You need to keep on top of your invoicing, ensure you pay the correct tax, and have the right insurance and a good accountant.

There are always challenging aspects to freelancing but hopefully these pointers will help guide you, whether freelancing becomes a career choice or just a stopgap while you search for a permanent job.

Be open-minded

In an ideal world, we would all love to be able to pick and choose the freelance work that we are offered. However, with the increase in designers choosing a freelance career, there is more competition than ever before for jobs.

Freelance jobs generally come up when companies need help on a specific stage of a project or have won more projects than the company can cope with. With this in mind, when they book a freelancer, they want to know that a designer can be brought in for a specific skill set and be able to work quickly and efficiently with little guidance. It's important for me to stress that the vast majority of freelance work is for designers with at least three or more years' post-graduation experience.

That said, if you are a junior interior designer, you might find that you inevitably begin your career freelancing at different companies while you find a permanent job.

Have a bracket

Companies will have a budget in mind on how much they want to spend, and not being lenient on your day rate can mean missing a whole week's work. Remember, you can always increase your day rate, so starting off on a lower rate can pay dividends in the long run.

Last minute

Most freelance jobs come through at short notice – a day or two, generally on a Thursday or Friday with a Monday start – so you have to make a decision quickly if you want to accept that work or risk not having anything. Short bookings might be extended, too. I have known week-long jobs that are extended until they become a six-month contract.

Most freelance jobs come through at <u>short notice</u> – so you have to make a decision quickly if you want to accept that work or risk not having anything.

Every contract offers opportunities

Consider the following scenario: you are an interior designer who loves working on the concept stage of the project but have had no work for a few weeks. A job helping out on a drawing pack for a supermarket comes along. It pays fairly well and is easy to commute to. When you reach the studio, you sit next to one of the senior designers, who is also a freelancer. Over the next few weeks you get to know each other and when your contract is coming to an end, they recommend you to a company they know who is recruiting. During your time at this studio, the director asks if you can show them your full portfolio. They are impressed by your work and say they will keep you posted if any concept work comes in.

By taking a short contract for a job that wasn't perfect, you have earned some money and opened up two other possible job leads.

$\longrightarrow$

Personal finances

If you are going to leave a permanent job to start freelancing, ensure you have had a quick audit of your personal finances. On the whole, freelancing rates are slightly more attractive than a permanent position. But there will be times when you won't be working, so have a fund that will cover bills. As a general rule, quiet times tend to be around the Christmas period and early January.

If you don't have much of a back-up fund, go through your bank statement and see what outgoings you can reduce. Look at your monthly expenses – could you save money on your mobile phone contract, cancel your gym membership, etc.?

Be patient

It may take you up to four weeks to find your first freelance role. When companies call me to find them a freelancer, they will always ask if a regular freelancer who I have placed with them previously is available, as they know the designer is familiar with the office set-up, their projects, and their way of working.

Companies can be wary if you haven't freelanced before as they like the reassurance that designers have a track record of freelancing, that they can work to strict deadlines, and that they're not overwhelmed by starting in a new company.

The way in is to strike while the iron's hot. If an opportunity comes your way, even if it's just for a few days, snatch it up!

The toolkit

The majority of companies will provide a computer and software; however, it is advantageous to have your own equipment during peak periods. In the summer, design agencies often don't have enough workstations, so they do often request freelancers who can work off their own laptop.

People buy people

Your work samples are your interview

The majority of freelance bookings will not require an interview as they are making a decision based on your portfolio. It is imperative your CV and portfolio are regularly updated with the companies you have freelanced at and projects you have had exposure to. Sometimes I find designers miss out on opportunities because their portfolios aren't up to date, despite being ideal for the freelance role.

Think about dividing your portfolio into several PDFs. Designers who have mixed project experience find this very handy. Also, you can tailor what PDFs you send out for various jobs. For example:

- *Overall portfolio: giving a snapshot of all of your work*
- *PDF focused purely on retail projects*
- *PDF focused purely on hospitality projects*
- *Technical PDF, showcasing your drawing ability*
- *Sketching/concept PDF*

Having multiple portfolios is very advantageous as it means you can send the relevant PDFs very quickly for certain jobs. When you start looking for freelance work, make sure you have changed your CV profile description (and LinkedIn profile) to reflect your freelance status, and be sure to sell your key skills and project experience.

People buy people

Your contacts are your network and 'people buy people'. A recommendation goes so much further than any other type of marketing. People love to recommend others as it makes them feel good and they want to help you.

Ensure you utilize all avenues to find work, from recruiters, your LinkedIn network, previous colleagues and friends in the design industry to job boards and approaching companies directly. Let people know you are available for work and what skills you can offer. Send a short email to them, apply to advertised freelance jobs, or send your CV and portfolio directly to companies you really admire with a summary of your skills, availability, and project experience.

Try and keep on top of this on a regular basis, even when you have work, as when quiet times inevitably hit, you want your name to be the first one everyone thinks of when projects start picking up.

53

→

Communication goes a long way

There have been a few times when a freelancer has been told to leave a contract early, and the company reports back they are not happy with the designer.

What tends to be the root cause of this problem is communication. The director is busy so they haven't taken the time to brief you properly on the project, which means you spend too much time trying to find files and working out what you need to do. In the meantime, unbeknown to you, the deadline is fast approaching.

In these scenarios you need to speak up before you start work. Find out exactly what is expected and in what time frame. If they don't have the time to brief you, find someone who can. As the old saying goes, bad news travels quicker than good, and in the design industry that couldn't be more true. If word spreads that you don't work quickly or it didn't work out, it can have a detrimental effect on your contracts going forward.

Overtime

Overtime is often not discussed. As a rule, freelancers are paid on a day rate and overtime is not paid. Companies expect some leniency on your hours and do not expect you to charge for the extra hour of overtime you have done.

We all know that designers can work long hours. If you are aware that it will be a late finish, then discuss the situation regarding overtime before you work the hours. Once you have worked the hours, it is unlikely overtime will be paid. In return for working a late night, sometimes companies will offer time in lieu.

Administration

This is the boring part to freelancing, but if admin is not kept on top of, it will cause big headaches in the long run. These are my top tops to stay organized:

- *Ensure you allocate time at least once a week to invoice companies, chase outstanding payments, record your expenses, and reconcile your bank statement.*

- *Put money aside each time you are paid, ideally in another account, to cover your tax bill. This will make your tax return at the end of the year a lot less stressful!*

- *Make sure you have the correct level of insurance, and make a note in your diary of the expiry date so you are ahead of the game to compare the market for the best deal.*

- *Sign up for accountancy software or a free app to make invoicing quick and easy, and to send out automatic reminders when payments are due.*

- *Always check who the correct person is to send your invoice to and ask if they require you to include their company's PO number.*

- *Diarize key dates for tax returns, corporation tax deadlines, and insurance expiry dates.*

- *Schedule in time for portfolio and CV updates, industry events to attend, and training sessions to upskill on software.*

- *Keep a digital folder with a copy of your passport, proof of address, incorporation certificate, emergency contact details, and insurance documents. These are all commonly requested by recruiters and companies when they book you for work.*

It may take up to four weeks for your first freelance role – <u>be patient.</u>

Chapter 6:

negotiating your salary

How to get paid what you deserve.

I struggle to think of anyone who is confident at negotiating their salary when they are in a job. It certainly seems easier to negotiate when you are offered a new role. But somehow, once we are in the door, have settled in and proved our worth, we feel the tables have turned.

One thing I think holds people back from asking their employer for a salary increase is the worry they will say no, that their job will suddenly be on the line, or it will cause a problem with the working relationship if it doesn't go your way. These are all completely understandable. However, imagine you are the director of the business and one of your hard-working employees comes to you with a pitch and valid reasons for wanting a pay increase. You would most likely admire them for doing this and give it serious consideration.

I hope the following steps will make you feel more prepared and confident in having these discussions. Using this method has rarely failed designers I have worked with in the past.

58

Before the meeting

Find your original job description/contract. If you don't have this, write a draft one of the job title and job duties you did when you started.

Write down what your current duties are. Compare what has changed and take a note of what responsibilities have increased. List any key projects you may have won or worked on, or projects you have finished ahead of schedule.

Have a look at job adverts online and compare your market value to other similar job roles. It is worth keeping a copy of these. Ring a recruiter to see what salary band they would consider you to be in for your level.

Imagine you're the director of the business – would you want to lose one of your <u>hard-working employees?</u>

During the meeting

There is no point in discussing a salary increase with someone who doesn't have the authority to give it. Ideally you should meet with the key decision-maker – the company director, HR manager, or both.

Treat your meeting as a pitch/presentation. Have your comparison job responsibilities and achievements to hand. A printout of key projects you have worked on is a good visual. In larger companies, directors may need to be reminded which projects you have been involved in, hence why a visual reference is key.

When the meeting starts, take the lead. Explain what your job title and responsibilities were when you joined the business, how they have changed, and the relationships you may have built with clients.

Go through any key projects you have been involved in and the part you have played in these. This may all sound extreme, but it is essential in putting your case forward and it is important to produce evidence. Nerves have a lovely way of making us lose our confidence, so having evidence in place will help guide you through the meeting and keep you on track.

It is important to talk about your future with the company, how you are invested in it, and what you would like to continue to do over the next year. Discuss taking on extra tasks, for example, planning social nights for the team, setting up a mentoring scheme, offering 'up-skilling' classes, contributing to the company's social media account, or working on small projects for a charity. These examples benefit the business and show you want to actively participate in the culture and future of the company.

Pitch the salary increase you are looking for. Do not apologize and hold your nerve to saying anything else. You have put your pitch forward, now allow them time to respond.

Other negotiations

An increase in money isn't the only thing you could consider asking for. Here are a few examples you might want to consider negotiating:

- *Flexible hours to work from home or attend a course*

- *Unpaid leave*

- *Course/training you would like to attend*

- *External mentor or coach*

- *Membership to a networking group or contribution towards attending industry events*

- *Lecturing at a university or running a workshop with students*

Anything that helps you reach your full potential stands to benefit your company as much as it does your career.

What happens next?

If the company comes back and isn't able to offer you a salary increase for whatever reason, be it budget restraints or they can only review it in six months' time, do not feel it has been a waste of effort. You can always go back asking for one of the alternative suggestions above. The directors are now fully aware of your contributions, skill set, and level. The ball is back in your court, and if you feel it is time to move on in order to achieve a higher salary, then at least you know you tried.

59

Chapter 7:

advice for junior interior designers

looking for work in the industry

———

Here, eight leading industry directors, who all specialize in the interior design sector, offer their advice for junior designers looking for work. This chapter covers how to make a lasting impression in an interview and what key skills designers should be demonstrating in their portfolio.

what general advice would you give a junior interior designer looking for work?

Howard Sullivan
YourStudio

'Try anything and everything. Internships get a bad name, but they're a really good way to broaden your experience beyond your college work. Do your research on the company interviewing you and arrive prepared. Shuffle the order of the case studies in your portfolio to fit with the practice you are presenting to. It's also always good to relate your work outwards by linking it with current influential case studies to show that you understand the broader context of design. Also, don't forget to do a couple of dry runs with a friend to get your presentation locked down.'

'Keep covering letters/introduction emails concise and to the point (we don't have time to read an essay!), and triple-check CVs for spelling mistakes. We get so many CVs from graduates that we have to narrow these down in some way. It sounds obvious, but don't send a sample portfolio which is over 15 Mb! If you get an interview with a company, do your research (and that doesn't just mean looking at their website). If you can, visit a project they have done and form an opinion yourself.'

George Gottl
FutureBrand UXUS

'Don't only show commercial projects but show your own point of view. If you feel you have a portfolio that is not extensive enough, then I highly recommend you include personal work; do a project for yourself so that we can understand what you represent, your own aesthetic, and your vision for how you feel design should be manifested.'

Mario Brown
Virgile + Partners

'Maintain and develop a solid knowledge of similar brands to keep up to date with current trends in communications, experiences, and events. Keep abreast of developments in cutting-edge architecture, design, digital, brand experience, and associated creative fields, maintaining an inquisitive and passionate interest.'

Lindsey Bean-Pearce
Dexter Moren Associates

'Make sure your portfolio is up to scratch. A good balance of interior plans and layouts, a good FF&E selection, and coloured graphical elevations are key. You should be able to tell a story with how you got to the end product. Sometimes the story is far more interesting than the end result.'

Shaun Clarkson
Shaun Clarkson ID

'Keep your focus succinct and directional. Show thought process, show you understand and can execute projects from start to finish.'

Marcus King
Dalziel & Pow

'Try everything. Make sure you get lots of work experience and/or internships to ensure that you're noticed and build relationships with people in the industry; recommendations are important. Utilize all your avenues to get an interview, from asking your contacts to going through agencies and networking at events. Always make sure you stay in contact with people even if they don't have a job offer at the time because businesses' requirements change day to day.'

Richard Greenleaf
HMKM

'Be flexible, try short-term freelance if it is offered, and be prepared to try new things. At the same time, try and be true to yourself. If your passion is fashion retail, don't work for an office design specialist as you may find yourself pigeonholed. For your next career move, you may find it difficult to jump out of office design into retail without a relevant track record.'

63

what do you look for when interviewing a junior interior designer?

Howard Sullivan
YourStudio

'A sense of passion and connection with what you've done and an eagerness to learn and develop. Junior team members are vital to the energy of a practice, so it's good to get a feeling that they're switched-on and connected in their interview.'

Jill Higgins
KKD

'A strong and varied skill base, enthusiasm and passion for design, initiative and intelligent thinking, willingness to get stuck in and show the same level of enthusiasm for both a mundane task and a more interesting one, and a balance of confidence and modesty. Someone who will bring and add something to our studio (from a personality and social perspective).'

Mario Brown
Virgile + Partners

'An excellent communicator and influencer. Someone who is team-oriented, enthusiastic, tenacious, resilient, and influential, to turn ideas into tangible and practical plans. A creative problem-solver who can approach client issues in new ways.'

George Gottl
Futurebrand UXUS

'We look for the designer's ability to express a concept or story in a physical environment. Whether it's a private or commercial space, you always need a big idea … for designers who are able to take an idea, and translate that into an atmosphere and a physical environment, to create a powerful overall look and tell a narrative through the space.'

Marcus King
Dalziel & Pow

'There is a lot of competition in the market between businesses like ours to find the best talent, as well as between graduates who are looking for a first opportunity to get into the industry. It is increasingly important that designers can demonstrate their interests and initiatives in order to stand out and differentiate themselves from the pack. For instance, I'm looking for graduate portfolios that are not just filled with the same projects as their classmates but show they have other work, interests, or practical experience to give them an edge. They need to ask themselves whether they are showing they want this enough and what makes them stand out?'

Lindsey Bean-Pearce
Dexter Moren Associates

'A portfolio showcasing their best and most interesting projects. When we interview, we want to see that person excited and passionate about design, so always start with your favourite project, give it some animation, and tell us the story behind it.'

Richard Greenleaf
HMKM

'Personality! Are they sparky, fun, outgoing, and ambitious? Do they talk well about their work? Are they passionate? As a junior, we are not expecting experience and depth of knowledge, but we are looking for someone who is ambitious and willing to learn.'

Shaun Clarkson
Shaun Clarkson ID

'The ability to adapt and move from one project to another is essential.'

65

what are the key skills junior interior designers should be demonstrating in their portfolio?

Howard Sullivan
YourStudio

'An interview is essentially a pitch. Your portfolio is your key tool, so edit, structure, and present it in a way that projects the best you. I love seeing how a project translates from brief to concept to final design. Conveying this well and succinctly is a good skill and will bring energy to your interview.'

Jill Higgins
KKD

'Graphic design sensibility, i.e. ability to layout a page nicely with white space and control … with a good range of 2D and 3D computer skills. Freehand sketching (if you have good skills). If you don't have strong skills, it is better not to include anything than weaken the overall standard of your overall portfolio … and use materials and colour!'

Mario Brown
Virgile + Partners

'Candidates should be able to support multiple design projects concurrently. An understanding of brands and communication of brands is essential with good ability to sketch, visualize, and communicate ideas fluently.'

Marcus King
Dalziel & Pow

'Creativity is key. I am always on the lookout for creative concepts full of ideas and original thinking and am especially interested in seeing how concepts are brought to fruition with style and relevant materials. Problem-solvers are equally valuable. It is important to see that a designer can not only identify a problem but has a hunger to solve it.'

Lindsey Bean-Pearce
Dexter Moren Associates

'A portfolio should be clearly set out: a simple layout and good typeface used throughout. Look on Behance at other people's portfolios if you're unsure. You'll get lots of ideas on layouts and fonts to use. Make sure to have a good mix of CAD, showcasing layouts, plans, elevations, and some key sections. Photoshop is essential. Use it to enhance your plans and to apply materials, shadows, and lighting to elevations to produce a really great graphic. If you are good at freehand sketching, then use it and include it. It's important to show all your skills and methods. Select your best projects to showcase. An interview shouldn't be long or boring, and you should feel comfortable chatting about your work and engaging us with your ideas.'

Richard Greenleaf
HMKM

'Good standards of CAD drawing and 3D modeling are essential, but most important for HMKM is an ability to communicate design ideas through sketching, so we like to see sketches or sketchbooks. All designers should be able to do a good CAD drawing or render; this is an expected minimum standard, so sketches are the only way a designer can demonstrate their personal design process, methodology, and thinking.'

Shaun Clarkson
Shaun Clarkson ID

'Illustrate your technical ability. Don't gab on too much, keep it short, and let the work speak. Expect to show your portfolio in 20 to 30 minutes.'

67

Chapter 9:

advice for middleweight interior designers

68

looking to move into a senior role

Three leading industry directors offer their advice on how middleweight designers can progress into senior designer roles. They explain what skills you need, how the roles differ, and what you can start doing now to be noticed.

70

how does the role of a senior interior designer <u>differ</u> from that of a middleweight interior designer in your design studio?

Michael Fern
EDGE

'The shift from middle to senior signifies more accountability in owning face-to-face communication. It involves stepping out of their comfort zone (aptitude) to presenting and justifying their work rather than just designing it. It's a whole new level of engagement, maturity, accountability, and responsibility. By the time you're in the position of senior designer, the expectation is that you can confidently lead the design of a project from start to completion, rather than delivering part of a project under the direction of others.

'By no means would we be expecting designers to do this in isolation. However, we would expect that the designer has a valuable role to play throughout the life of the project and will amass a great deal of tacit knowledge that places them in a pivotal role in ensuring a project can be finished as well as it has started. Creating a clear thread that runs all the way through.'

Tom Edington
YourStudio

'A senior designer is not only expected to lead their own projects, but to have the awareness to help guide others, even if they are not necessarily resourced with that client/job. We expect a senior to lead across two to four projects at any one time. Whereas a middleweight has a more focused workload, we try to get seniors leading on one project then being resourced on another under a senior.'

Jill Higgins
KKD

'There is lots of overlap between a middleweight and senior role, so we try to approach it on an individual basis according to each designer's strengths. Some middleweights have amazing client skills but are still developing their design skills, and others have the technical or conceptual skills but lack the confidence to present. Consequently, the main difference between a senior and middleweight designer tends to be the size of projects they are leading. I would also expect a senior to manage a client independently, whereas a middleweight would normally need a little bit more top-level support.'

71

72

what <u>skills</u> and <u>experience</u> do you look for when you are considering <u>promoting</u> or <u>hiring</u> a middleweight interior designer to a senior position?

Jill Higgins
KKD

'A strong skill base and broad understanding across the whole design process, from conceptual thinking through to technical detail, is essential. But equally important are their people skills. They must have the right personality to nurture young designers, work with and support seniors, as well as beginning to manage clients. Being able to see a designer's potential and ambition is also a must. Middleweight level is the point where you can really identify the individuals who can go further within the industry, so we would be looking out for those we believe have the most potential.'

Tom Edington
YourStudio

'Being able to demonstrate their ability to lead a project is key. We would expect them to be experienced at managing their own workload and deliverables, while being able to oversee some of the more junior team. Their client skills should have matured to such a level where we are comfortable with them being able to lead client communications and presentations.'

Michael Fern
EDGE

'Promotion is always based on a mixture of aptitude and attitude at EDGE. Mid to senior is recognition that you've honed both your practical and professional skills, which then enable you to be comfortable in owning more of the conceptual and delivery capability on a project.'

73

what can a middleweight interior designer <u>start doing now</u> to be noticed for <u>promotion</u> or <u>prepare</u> for a senior interior designer role?

Tom Edington
YourStudio

'This is a big step up in responsibility. It's when a designer moves from being managed to self-managing and taking responsibility for others. You'd expect them always to come with solutions to problems and not rely so much on their seniors. You'd want to see them taking a measured approach to their work, keeping the energy but being more considered around the studio, starting to show their ability to be a calm head in a storm. As with all our staff we want to see them hungry for growth, up for a challenge, and being proactive around the studio.

'I'd expect them to start taking a greater responsibility for projects, helping and mentoring others, and adding value across the board. By responsibility I don't mean glory. It's even doing the small jobs, like helping clear up after meetings, that really gets noticed. As a company we always want to be challenged. This brings the best out of our creativity, so we expect them to bring a point of view to all conversations.'

Michael Fern
EDGE

'Think about ways of making your presence felt on a project. As leaders of design studios, we rely on open communication from the team to ensure that we deliver work that answers the brief, creates value for our clients, and raises awareness of our capabilities as a creative design studio. Envision projects like vehicles to help you on your journey. A mixture of fast and slow, moving to widen your experience and hone your skills. If you see something coming along, make sure you ask to be part of it. And make yourself "sticky" on a project so you become indispensable through your knowledge, insight, and/ or skills to ensure you stay with the project all the way through. There are lots of designers out there who know how to develop an idea but don't know how to deliver it, so it's important to make sure you learn from the delivery of projects … It's often where success or failure happens. All the above is trying to illustrate that we're wanting to buy into you as an individual and not just as a Mac/CAD monkey. Future success relies on thinkers, not just doers.'

Jill Higgins
KKD

'The most important thing they could do is start to take more responsibility and show initiative in the jobs that they do. They also need to try and demonstrate their ability to nurture and guide less experienced members of the team, as well as showing their time management and multitasking skills. It's also good for them to display an awareness of the business side of the industry and, as always, their passion for the subject and jobs they're taking on!'

75

when you have <u>interviewed</u> interior designers in the past, what has made particular candidates <u>stand out</u> from the crowd?

Tom Edington
YourStudio

'Passion, doing their research, their attitude, and obviously talent. You always want a future employee to show passion as that way you know they are going to bring something extra to the team. You'd be amazed at the amount of people we interview who don't do their research on our company. It's just disappointing, and it immediately makes you judge them as lazy (which isn't a trait you want to portray). Someone's attitude counts more than you can imagine. You want positive people in the studio: someone who brings an energy. A positive, polite, and team player attitude is a must for me. Finally, talent. Talent isn't something you can just magic up. It's natural but it can also be worked on and honed. Understand your strengths and weaknesses so you can always improve.'

Michael Fern
EDGE

'We really love interviews where you get an insight into how designers think and how they apply this to their work. Finished photos are great, but design is so subjective it's sometimes not best to focus on the finished work (unless it's something that you're truly proud of). Instead, bring sketchbooks and design work that shows how an idea has evolved from inception through development to completion. Be clear on what the brief was and how you personally helped shape the solution. We also like to throw in a few killer questions, such as, "What's your biggest failure and what did you learn from it?" It's a genius question for getting to the real person rather than the interview veneer.

'Overall, it's clear that if you're looking to progress from middleweight interior designer to senior interior designer, make sure to clearly demonstrate your abilities, show your passion, and hone your talent. Don't be afraid to be proactive and really put your effort into helping and making yourself indispensable.'

Jill Higgins
KKD

'The main qualities that make a candidate stand out are their talent and finesse – the desire to do the most beautiful work at all times and having the work ethic to support that. We look for individuals who demonstrate a natural business acumen and show emotional intelligence when it comes to working with other designers and the ability to "read a room" when meeting with clients. It's also nice to see individuals with a quiet confidence and ambition while still acknowledging their need to learn and the areas they need to develop.'

Chapter 9:

advice for senior interior designers

looking to take the step up to an associate role

Quick-thinking, creative vision, and developing an external focus are some of the key attributes employers are looking for in a senior designer wanting to make the leap to associate.

80

what do you look for when interviewing a senior interior designer for an associate role?

Siu-Lan Choi
Household

'Quick-thinkers, problem-solvers, good communicators, able to juggle and, of course, super creatives!'

Paul Digby
HMKM

'A good senior designer will be honing their all-round ability: total concept to completion skills. You would be expected to demonstrate executing a medium-to-large-scale project, helping set the creativity and seeing it through to the finish within a team. Verbal skills in the presentation of this work are as important as the creativity itself. It would be expected that they will be presenting to future clients, so clear and well-delivered creative storytelling is essential.'

Lewis Allen
Portland Design

'Having an awareness of the world, what's happening to the sectors we work in, and what forces are shaping them helps in understanding how the direction of creative vision influences opportunities and challenges for our clients. The importance of effective communication skills, articulation, inspiring ideas, and language are paramount throughout the design process.'

Andy Smith
Twelve Studio

'Someone I can work closely with, trust, and have a connection with. Bringing an all-round skill set to guide and advise a junior team, with experience in all stages of process from concept through to delivery. Even if their strength lies in one area, having a wide range of experience across different sectors and aesthetics is really helpful, especially as the nature of our work is so broad. An ability to demonstrate working to tight timelines and limited budgets is always advantageous as well as working on luxury projects or those with longer lead times.'

Jill Higgins
KKD

'A fun, nice person to work with who has a point of view, and who is going to bring something different to the studio and make the role their own.'

81

how does the role of an associate differ from that of a senior interior designer?

Siu-Lan Choi
Household

'Delegation is key! The transition from senior to associate is often difficult because as creatives we naturally want to do it all, but the jump is essentially a leap into leadership, bigger-picture understanding, and accepting that it might take longer for someone else to do it but, sometimes, that's what needs to be done. Being able to understand the strengths and weaknesses of the design team, not only for the benefit of each project and role within that but also from a nurturing perspective. Actively supporting and identifying ways to grow individuals is another aspect that demonstrates great leadership.'

Andy Smith
Twelve Studio

'Someone who can think for themselves, is self-sufficient, and is able to juggle lots of things at the same time.'

Jill Higgins
KKD

'At associate level you should be able to deal with both creative pitches and presentations, and handle difficult client situations, combining being a talented designer but also an intelligent thinker. Being able to work collaboratively (both internally and externally with clients) is integral to client management and business acumen in identifying new leads, opportunities, and grow existing business. The ability to "do" as well as lead is important. Even if you are not an expert in every bit of software, you should have a good understanding in order to manage the team.

'Experience and a passion for nurturing young talent, in a way to guide and teach (not to stifle) creativity; there is no room for ego at KKD, and even less so at a higher level, so equally you must have the ability to constructively criticize and critique work to maintain the quality of what we do.'

Lewis Allen
Portland Design

'It is so important to build relationships with clients as the role of an associate is to offer insight, analysis, and opinions about a broad range of topics, not just design. This extends to being commercially savvy in owning the business objectives on efficiency and sectoral insights.'

Paul Digby
HMKM

'Generally an associate would be expected to work across several projects. They would be the client's liaison and the primary knowledge base. A senior designer would already be managing the more junior team members. An associate, as well as being the team leader, should be seen as a mentor to equip other seniors who want to further their design careers. HMKM would also expect an associate to have a strong understanding of the market and category, be very aware of global trends, and have a decent understanding of brand.'

84

what can senior interior designers start <u>doing now</u> to be noticed for a <u>promotion</u> or to <u>prepare</u> for an associate role?

Siu-Lan Choi
Household

'Learn to deal with curveballs – after all, life is full of them, especially agency life! Don't let it panic you; think on your feet and demonstrate agility and adaptability. The way you respond to a situation is what other designers will learn from, so staying positive when things don't go to plan is an important skill to master.'

Andy Smith
Twelve Studio

'Gently take the reins on projects so associates/directors suddenly find themselves with extra time to dedicate to company matters, e.g. new business.'

Lewis Allen
Portland Design

'Developing an external focus (beyond the internal dynamics of the business), such as clients and industry events, broadens horizons. We expect you to express opinions and demonstrate your ability to give constructive analysis on anything and everything. Start taking responsibility, giving input, and becoming accountable for projects and other business activities (be it IT or social media). As a manager you are expected to lead on brief developments, planning, and delivering projects. I would advise senior designers to seek out internal leadership in becoming a mentor to others. By working across sectors and teams you will enhance your experience of other disciplines and work processes.'

Paul Digby
HMKM

'Visibly stepping up to challenges is always a plus. Taking on additional responsibilities is always welcome to take the pressure out of a situation. Creative frustrations and problem-solving often arise in our industry. I'm always happy to see seniors put themselves forward for the tricky tasks that help the wider team and ensure a project is delivered to the highest standard.'

85

Chapter 10:

the in–

—crowd

As you will no doubt know by now, interior design is so much more than picking fabric patterns and paint colours. It offers up a vast array of challenging and diverse career paths. Here, I've interviewed a wide variety of designers to give you an insight into just some of the different professional journeys out there as well as snapshots into the day-to-day lives of the people who are on them.

The designers included here are all at varying stages of their careers, from juniors to directors, and have worked on multiple projects, all taking slightly different routes to get to where they are today. Whether they're running their own design consultancies, have moved from permanent jobs into freelancing, or are now working client-side, I hope their stories inspire you and remind you that every opportunity you take will only enhance your career.

Alex Greenaway

Creative director
OpenLab

88

Career overview

My degree had a sandwich year in industry, which really helped shape things for me. Through a chance opportunity, I followed up and secured a placement for a large experiential agency. A friend knew that I was into design and his neighbour was a creative director and passed on his details. The company had a broad scope of international projects for commercial brands but also some interesting cultural projects. One was the theatrical production and live ceremony for the transfer of sovereignty of Macau from Portugal to China. The opportunity showed me early on that a career can and will be determined by a mix of good fortune, opportunity, and hard work. You can make up for some of this by chasing your own opportunities, with creative ambition, but when starting out – it's all hard work.

My placement turned into my first role after graduation, which opened my eyes, and was a long way from the day to day of my studies. I had more interest in the creation of interior environments than furniture and product design, but

it served me well as a foundation for what was to come. You will find that it is your personality as much as your studies that will shape your career. I also began to see the nature of a deadline-driven industry – a warm welcome to the reality of commercial design and creativity!

In your first years you will see so much, make mistakes, do the boring things, stay late, etc. But you should make sure to understand the tools of your trade. These can really set you apart from your peers. It can be easy to go unnoticed in a busy studio environment, so get involved – be confident, but not overly. Talking about ideas and having an opinion is the way forward to your development, and any good studio will promote this. But remember to listen as well. This is how it began for me, pulling together presentations and learning how to unpack ideas for a client from a creative theme. Ultimately, this led me to understand the balance and principles between creativity, technical execution, and practical thinking. The technical and detailed understanding only comes with experience over time, but if it is something you love, work at it and be the best you can be.

I stayed in my first role for six years, moving from a technical draftsman across to a more creative role, shaping ideas within the studio and being exposed to clients, which allowed me to be comfortable as a confident 'all-rounder'.

The next ten or so years, I chose to freelance and went on a mission to work with some of the best creative practices and studios in London. I had some good and some bad experiences, but quickly understood to never judge a book by its cover. Many agencies aren't what you perceive until you have worked inside them, and it forced me to quickly conceptualize and bring ideas to life in the most flexible

way possible as a hired hand. I ended up staying in some big agencies that were turning over a huge amount of projects. As I accumulated brand and project knowledge; my role became easier to creatively lead and was more project driven. I was able to put together different creative skills in graphic design, 3D environments, and digital. As new briefs landed, we were intensely prototyping and using this to inform the next. As challenges arose, I knew that I could learn something new and take it to the next, covering retail, specialist automotive environments, and live experiences.

→

Alex Greenaway
portfolio excerpts

90

Left:
Redbull Racing – MK7
brand experience
Velocity Experience, 2018

Left:
Diageo, main bar,
World Class Haus, Berlin
TBA Group, 2018

Right:
Jaguar F-Type
Global Press Reveal
Paris Motor Show
Imagination, 2012

Right:
Taste of Tanqueray
brand experience
TBA Group, 2018

With some of the higher-profile agency projects came big brands and budgets as well as flagship projects for your portfolio – a big prize, but it came with pressure. While tight timelines and higher stakes mentally test you, they can also work to bring out everyone's best. That's when the talent around you unites into this working experience for the detail on a live project. It can lead to some of the most fulfilling projects you may have in your lifetime, and I've had a few of those. Although it was unpleasant at the time, it's what's required to bring these crazy projects to life. It's what makes the design push boundaries and challenge what other industries can be about. I remember when we launched a luxury SUV to the world's media. We had a ridiculous amount of fanfare with kinetic LED walls and driving it through an in-door waterfall with a reservoir we had built, following an intense project timeline. I nearly cried. But it's something I look back on with pride. There can be an intensity to creativity that can be very fulfilling. It defines who you can be professionally. Equally there must be balance and I wasn't afraid to turn my back on that constant level of output. You can burn out and it stops you from producing your best work.

Sometimes magic can start to happen <u>by accident.</u>

A typical day

I always carve out time in my schedule where I can get clear headspace to create what I feel the right direction is to steer a creative project. As I have gotten more senior, making sure we are spending the right amount of design time on projects and making decisions from a more commercial point of view becomes increasingly important. Sometimes magic can start to happen by accident and giving people the space to do that so that an idea can develop is integral to what I do now. Knowing when to push further and polish the details is key. Creative direction: part designer, part creative manager, part businessperson.

What do you love about being an interior designer?

I've worked across several industries and created varying physical environments, but whatever it is, the moment that you see something that has been fabricated into a physical form it creates a buzz. Seeing things in the flesh for the very first time gives a nervous gratification. It brings an infectious excitement to all who have been involved in its creation. It's part geekery, pure creationary, and a unique feeling which never changes.

What advice would you give to interior designers starting out in their career?

Be a geek. The world is owned by geeks. Read about great projects — and I don't just mean on Instagram. Look at who has achieved greatness outside of your immediate creative area of expertise and take inspiration from this.

Don't be afraid to throw away an idea — if it is one of your first few ideas, someone else has already thought of it — go again. Dig deeper.

Follow up on everything that could have an opportunity behind it and don't be too disappointed with rejection. It means that another opportunity will take its place.

Make yourself extremely useful in as many areas as possible. Particularly in anything that could help form a good idea.

93

Left:
Red Bull Racing Paddock
Club Lounge concept
Velocity Experience, 2018

Alex Vick

Senior designer
Event Communications

Specialist in:

3D design

Title of your degree:

BA (Hons)
Interior Architecture

Career overview

I graduated in 2011 and after one of my lecturers at Cardiff put in a good word about me to the museum design company Casson Mann, I applied for a job as a junior designer there as soon as I graduated. After a couple of interviews, I got the job and was very much thrown in at the deep end. The first project I worked on was a permanent exhibition at the National Maritime Museum for the Nelson, Navy, Nation gallery. It was a very fast project turnaround, and I played a key role in helping to design the exhibition. Before I knew it, I was on site seeing my first designs in the flesh.

I then went on to a project in Bologna called Fondazione MAST – an international cultural institution for art, technology, and innovation. We provided the concept for the exhibition, which was then built in 2013. In just over a year at Casson Mann I already had two built projects under my belt, which really helped me progress to a middleweight designer role in 2015.

After working on a feasibility project at the V&A, I went on to work on one of the most notable projects of my career so far, the refurbishment of Hintze Hall at the Natural History Museum in London. This project lasted around four years and was completed in June 2017. I very much had a key role in designing the museum and was given a lot of freedom by a colleague who was leading the project. It was an extremely prestigious project to work on, and I saw it through from pitch to completion. I really enjoyed the on-site experience, seeing my showcase designs in such a beautiful and important building was really exciting and knowing that they would be in the museum for years and years to come was a great feeling. During the Hintze Hall project there were moments I worked on other projects such as Lascaux (Centre International de l'Art Pariétal, Montignac) and La Cité du Vin, Bordeaux. Both projects were completed in 2016.

→

Alex Vick
portfolio excerpts

Left:
Concept visual
for Showtown –
Blackpool Museum
Casson Mann, 2018

Left:
Concept visual for
MAST – International
Cultural Institution for
Art, Technology and
Innovation, Bologna
Casson Mann, 2013

Right:
Concept sketches
for Hintze Hall –
Natural History
Museum, London
Casson Mann, 2018

Right:
Concept visual
for Nottingham
Castle Museum
and Art Gallery
Casson Mann, 2018

Personal time is so valuable.

The other key project I worked on was at the Nottingham Castle Museum and Art Gallery, which consisted of six large galleries and interpretation in the grounds. Some of the galleries were traditional art galleries and others were media-focused galleries, such as an immersive Robin Hood experience and an exhibition about rebellion in Nottingham. This project is planned to be completed in 2020.

When I was promoted to senior designer in 2018, I initially worked on a small retail project at Harrods Fine Wines & Spirits Rooms, which involved a series of sensory media tables where customers could smell different flavour components in various wines and whiskies. This was a fast turnaround project that finished in summer 2018. I then went on to work on Blackpool Museum Project where I played a key role in coming up with a fresh concept for the exhibition. This new concept used the idea of backstage and VIP to give visitors a different perspective on all the famous performers and rich history that Blackpool has had and still has to this day. This project is also planned to be completed in 2020.

It was during this project I decided that I wanted to become a freelance exhibition and museum designer. The main reason being I wanted more time to focus on painting. I had been running an art business selling my artwork since I was about fifteen years old. I freelanced for around five months before the company I work for currently, Event Communications, offered me a permanent job with one non-working day a week for me to focus on my art. I started work on a large pavilion in Dubai for Expo 2020, and I'm currently working on a visitor experience project for Carlsberg at their HQ in Copenhagen.

A typical day

A typical day might involve meetings with the project team, which usually consists of a content designer, graphic designer, and 3D designers. As my expertise is 3D design, I then evolve the design on a CAD program.

What do you love about being an interior designer?

I love the opportunity that I get to work on diverse projects. Some are more traditional exhibitions, which use no media, but you get to see the amazing back-of-house collections, which the public never get to see. Other projects might be more media based, so there are no objects, but you get to be more creative in terms of your design input. Some projects focus on parts of history, so you must become a specialist in that subject to be able to design an exhibit which responds to the story of the object.

98

What advice would you give to interior designers starting out in their career?

It's a small world and an even smaller industry, so stay in everyone's good books!

A lot of design is about dealing with people and it's always tempting to put on a front, especially when meeting clients, but I always think you should be yourself. A lot of the time that's exactly why clients come back to you and want to work with you again.

Being dedicated and passionate about design doesn't mean working all hours and weekends. Personal time is so valuable. A lot of the time, ideas come to me during my down time.

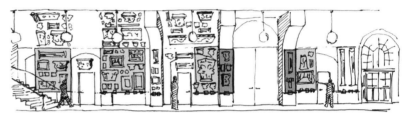

Top:
Concept sketch and visual for Burlington House,
Royal Academy of Arts, London
Casson Mann, 2013

Alice Richardson

Junior interior designer
The Yard Creative

Specialist in:

Food and beverage, retail, and experiential

Title of your degree:

BA (Hons) Interior Architecture and Design

Career overview

I started off my career with an internship at a small design agency, which I returned to after graduation. I didn't stay there long, as I realized I wasn't being challenged and there was little opportunity for career progression. Since joining The Yard Creative, I have been exposed to so many different types of projects and have worked on every part of the design process. I have also been challenged in so many ways and I can see how much I have developed since joining. There is a clear career progression for me – these reasons are why I accepted a job here! When I first started out, I often felt like I wasn't properly designing (the idea of design I had in my head when I graduated, which in hindsight might have been a bit far-fetched!), but I was actually doing more than I realized. Design can be even in the smallest bits, from working out a detail to specifying the right furniture. And all of these small tasks have given me the confidence and knowledge I have today!

→

Alice Richardson
portfolio excerpts

Left:
Sketches and finished photography for Twenty3C bike shop, Wembley
The Yard Creative, 2019

Right:
HOB Salons,
Brent Cross
Innovare Design, 2017

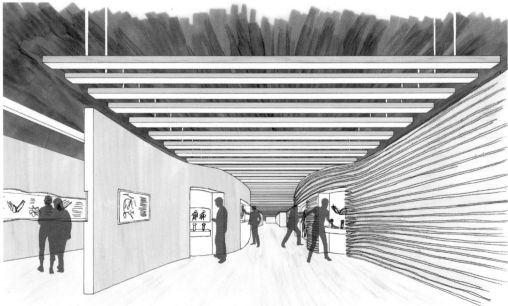

Right:
University Final
Project, Museum of
the Human Body
Nottingham Trent,
2017

A typical day

Being a junior means a lot of variation. Sometimes I'll be focused on one project, doing everything from talking to clients and going to meetings to doing detail drawings and visuals. Other times, I will be working across multiple projects in one week, supporting my colleagues with their projects, with tasks ranging from specifying furniture and finishes or updating drawings to researching trends or designing a specific area.

What do you love about being an interior designer?

Every day brings a new adventure. I'm always learning! I love being able to create something new that customers will be able to experience, and I'm always up for a design challenge. At the moment, I am loving how varied each project that I'm working on is! Being in London means there are lots of design talks, shows, and exhibitions going on, so it's nice to go out and learn about new things in the design world and get inspiration from as many people as I can.

Unfamiliarity is a good thing.

What advice would you give to interior designers starting out in their career?

Don't get comfortable! Always push yourself and don't be afraid to ask for certain kinds of work. Unfamiliarity is a good thing: in the end it will make you a better designer.

Left:
K+K Street Food,
Sri Lankan restaurant,
Boxpark Croydon
The Yard Creative, 2019

Charlotte Hodges

Freelance interior designer
Free Form ID

Specialist in:

Hospitality and retail

Title of your degree:

*BA (Hons)
Interior Design*

Career overview

When I graduated, my goal was to find a job in London as soon as possible. I created my CV and portfolio and sent it out to over fifty interior design and architectural studios in London. I secured two interviews in August and September: one for a permanent position in the interiors department of an architectural studio and one for an unpaid internship. Having been offered both roles, I accepted the offer for the permanent position. My focus in this job was a residential property. I was involved in the concept, visuals, and the technical drawing pack. Although the role wasn't in the sector I wanted to work in, my first job gave me a really good grounding in the industry and some important experience in working for a professional design practice.

After three years in this job, I contacted a recruiter to try and find my next job at a studio that was active in a sector I did want to work in: retail and hospitality. They found me a great job at a small interiors practice, and I spent nearly two years there gaining valuable retail and hospitality experience. At this point I felt confident to pursue a role in my dream sector – fashion retail design. With the help of a recruiter once again, I secured a role at a leading studio in the field.

Unfortunately, after three months and during my probation period, I was made redundant. Although redundancies aren't uncommon in the fast-changing world of interior design, at the time this felt like the worst thing that had ever happened to me. I decided to freelance in order to still be paid while I looked for my 'perfect' permanent job.

My freelancing career has lasted over three years, and I couldn't be more thankful to have been made redundant. In this time, I have worked at over eight different design companies, starting off working in short-term contracts and later moving on to longer-term contracts at established studios. My latest contract was with an amazing boutique hospitality company who were primarily working for Virgin Voyages on their first cruise ship.

→

Charlotte Hodges
portfolio excerpts

108

Left:
Medicine finishes

Left:
Colombian food
moodboard

Top and right:
Concept sketches for
York Art Gallery
Lustedgreen, 2015

110

This was a new challenge for me as there are so many rules and regulations that don't apply to typical hospitality projects.

During my first year of freelancing, I worked under an umbrella company that organized the financial and tax side of things, which initially gave me more headspace to concentrate on my work. However, after speaking to other freelancers, I made the decision to start my own limited company called Free Form ID. Starting my own business ultimately meant I had more control over my finances and taxes.

The prospect of designing a gastro pub by myself was overwhelming but an exciting challenge! This project included: designing the concept, helping with new branding, creating a technical drawing pack and schedules, and attending site visits up until completion. Having completed my first project for Royal Holloway, they then asked me to help them with two further projects: a bar/nightclub and a refurbishment of their student union.

After finishing my first job for Royal Holloway, a Columbian street food business contacted me to deliver a permanent outdoor food kiosk for them. Having accepted the job, I worked with the client to create a brand-new concept, created a technical drawing pack, found a contractor, and attended site visits until completion.

A typical day

I am currently working on another project for the Columbian street food kiosk client in North London. This involves me working from home and creating a technical drawing pack, looking at sourcing materials that work within the budget, and going to site. One difference this project has involved is that I have had to source the contractor, which is typically the project manager's role. This is another challenge to make sure you find a good contractor!

What do you love about being an interior designer?

Being able to see your ideas come to life. It is a huge buzz to go to site to see how the project comes together after working on it for so long.

Work hard and good things will happen.

What advice would you give to interior designers starting out in their career?

Work hard and good things will happen! If you put the hours in now, you will be rewarded later on.

Left:
Italian restaurant for
Virgin Voyages
Volume Creative 2018-19

Ed Plumb

Founder and director
Studio Found

Specialist in:
Hospitality and retail

Title of your degree:
BA (Hons)
Interior Design

Career overview

Graduating in 2008 was not ideal. Looking for my first job shortly after the financial crash was challenging to say the least. Most agencies were downsizing and not on the lookout for fresh-faced designers straight out of uni. Following the New Designers show, I was offered a job at an events company. It was not really the sector I was interested in and was based out in Brentford, therefore far from the inspiring design job I had dreamt of as my first role. Nevertheless, it was a job, and I put my all into it, creating designs for Red Bull Racing and The O2. I did not really enjoy it mostly due to the lack of a mentor and constantly feeling out of my depth. However, in hindsight I learnt a lot, and while many of my peers were forced to take jobs outside of the industry, I was at least designing.

In six months, the events company went bust, and I was back without a job in a challenging time for the industry. I spent four hours every day calling design practices and architects trying to get in the door. Eventually after three months I was offered some freelance work at Kinnersley Kent Design (KKD). My old tutor's wife was a senior designer at the company, and they were looking for a junior to help with a large design project for House of Fraser. The position was initially for two weeks, but I ended up being there for six years and working on a huge range of projects, which included a number of shops at the Tower of London and Hampton Court Palace, managing the roll-out of womenswear brand Mint Velvet, creating designs for a luxury department store in Beirut, and many more inspiring and educating projects. It also included a four-month spell working in KKD's Dubai office, which was great fun. I look back at my time at KKD very fondly. It helped create the solid foundations I still rely on now. And the team there was, and is, very supportive of the next generation of designers.

After six years at KKD I was getting itchy feet, but rather than jump to another agency, I decided I wanted to feed my love of furniture. KKD was very supportive and allowed me to

work three days a week for them while I set up a company sourcing and selling mid-century furniture to designers for use in projects, as well as private customers. While running this company, my partner and I bought a house and spent two years renovating it, much of which I did myself while still doing some occasional freelancing at KKD.

When I completed my house renovations, I decided to get fully back into design and took a freelance job at the design arm of SFD as a senior designer. This turned into a full-time role, and I completed some great projects there. Unfortunately, the design arm of SFD closed, and it was then that I decided it was time to focus on generating my own work and set up Studio Found. I had built up great relationships with several clients at SFD and as there was no longer a design studio element to their business, I was able to work with these clients, which is how I completed my first projects as Studio Found.

$\longrightarrow$

Ed Plumb
portfolio excerpts

114

Left:
Clyde restaurant
Studio Found 2018

Left:
Brother2Brother store
OUR HOUSE Design
Studio, 2016-17

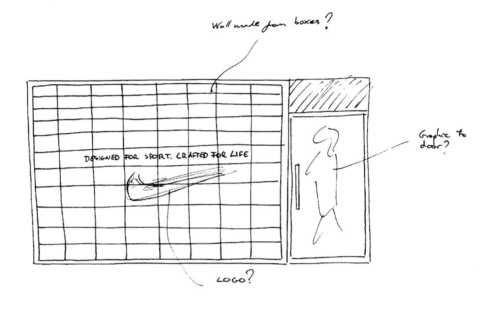

Wall made from boxes?

Graphic to door?

DESIGNED FOR SPORT. CRAFTED FOR LIFE

LOGO?

Layered?

Graphic?

Man display?

Boxes?

Top and right:
Development sketches

Treat every job as an opportunity to learn.

Studio Found is a small agency. The team is typically three to five people and combines interior designers, architects, and graphic designers. Our portfolio consists mainly of retail and hospitality projects, which includes 2D and 3D design but also some residential and commercial architecture. Our current projects include a large shop for Wedgwood and Waterford Crystal at Harrods; a 4,000-square-metre mixed-use new building in Essex, which incorporates residential, workspace and commercial uses; a roastery and barista school in Peckham for a London-based coffee brand; as well as several residential projects.

A typical day

Very varied to be honest, as we are a small agency. I do a lot of the design work myself as well as the more technical side on top of managing the team. We have a project finishing in the next few weeks, so I'll be spending a lot of time this week visiting the shop fitter's factory and Harrods to check on progress. I also have several new business meetings and a new project brief that needs working on.

What do you love about being an interior designer?

I love how many sectors require interior design and how ultimately it all comes down to one thing: the way a space makes you/the customer/the homeowner feel. If you understand this, it is possible to work across the various sectors that interior design affects.

What advice or guidance would you give to interior designers starting out in their career?

Treat every job as an opportunity to learn.

Learn to draw properly (it will always impress potential employers) and practise your sketching whenever you can (try to sketch an idea before using a 3D program).

Accept that not all jobs will be exciting, but they will teach you something however mundane they seem.

Be patient. I look back at my career so far and, with hindsight, can see how each step has helped to develop my skills. The beauty of our industry is that it is very varied, and everyone can find their niche.

Top right:
Fishmonger sketches

117

Jenny Lau-Fuller

Senior retail design manager
URW

Specialist in:
Brand experience design

Title of your degree:
BA (Hons)
Design and Applied Arts:
Interior Design

Career overview

When I graduated in 2000, there were not many interior design positions in Scotland, so I initially worked as a freelance production designer based in Wasps Artists Studios in Glasgow. Jobs included BAFTA Scotland Awards Event, theatre set design, build and scenic painting, and art department assistant on films. I supplemented my freelance with a part-time job at Habitat selling furniture. While there I contacted Tom Dixon and secured a work placement week in London at the Habitat Design Studio. I used the week to set up some London interviews and from that I secured a junior retail designer position at Rodneyfitch. This was my first introduction to the world of retail design. Projects included shopping malls in South East Asia and retail stores.

After a year I moved to Design International, an architecture firm specializing in European shopping malls for Eurocommercial, and I was the main interior designer, which gave me client-facing and site experience on commercial projects, including Le Passage du Havre in Paris, Carosello and San Guiliano in Milan, and La Favorita in Mantua, working with a European team. In 2003 I moved to FITCH, a leading global brand consultancy, which is where I earned my design stripes. It was a highly creative and fast-paced studio with a focus on freehand sketching, which honed my skills. I worked in multi-disciplinary teams on international projects for flagship retail stores, events, workspaces, design guidelines, and brand spaces, including Apple, Qatar Asian Games, Aquascutum, Hackett, Hammerson, Nokia, Russian Post, and Vodafone.

After several years and no opportunity for promotion, I set up my own design consultancy. The concept of freelancing appealed to me at the time so I could travel in between jobs. It built my confidence and challenged me much more than sitting at the same desk every day.

Specializing in brand experience, I worked with a range of creative and commercial businesses, including 20.20, Imagination, Interbrand, Ogilvy, Selfridges, and Universal Design Studio. I worked on many projects, including Al-Futtaim, Arsenal Emirates Stadium, Banamex, Crew Clothing, Dubai Festival City, HSBC, Façonnable, Fallon, Land Rover, Liverpool FC Anfield Stadium, Kiddicare, Mazda, Motorola, Orient Express, Samsung, TAG Heuer, and TUI.

In 2010 I took an in-house contract role as a retail design manager on the development of Westfield Stratford City. A £1.45 billion development across 1.9 million square feet. At the time I had wanted to find a permanent role. The longer-term contract offered income security without commitment, and it was a great opportunity. After opening, the team streamlined, and I went back to design agency freelancing and as a consultant design manager at Selfridges. I worked on luxury brand projects in the Oxford Street flagship store, as well as regional sites and in-house projects.

Jenny Lau-Fuller
portfolio excerpts

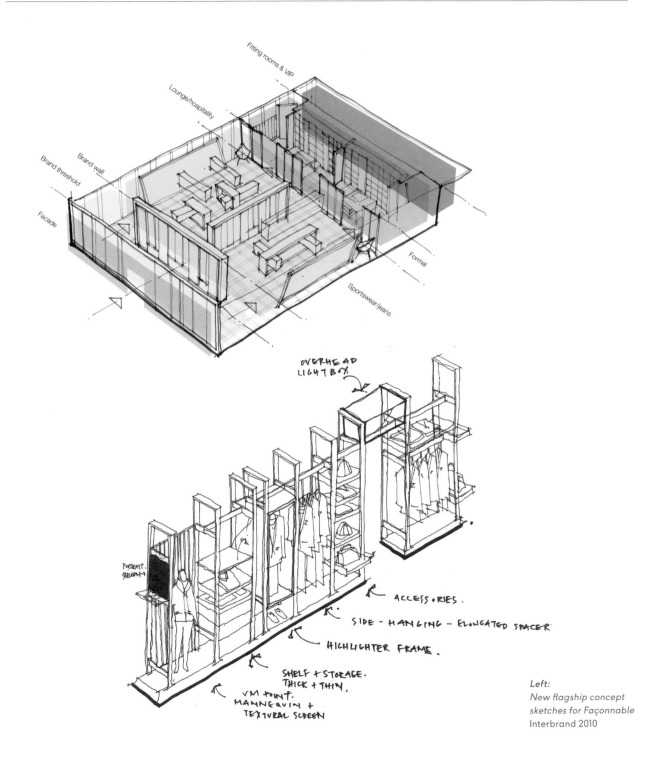

Left:
New flagship concept
sketches for Façonnable
Interbrand 2010

Right:
Liverpool FC
International Lounge
20.20, 2012

Right:
Westfield Stratford
City shopping centre
2011

What advice would you give to interior designers starting out in their career?

Network and make connections in the industry — be memorable.

Learn from your mentors and peers. Respect their skill and experience.

Don't be afraid to make mistakes but make sure you learn from them.

Be curious and ask questions; everyone has a valid opinion and voice.

122

Far left:
Façade drawing,
Hackett flagship
store, Sloane Street,
London
FITCH, 2004

Then I decided it was time to take an in-house permanent role, and I had a few interesting options, including both at Selfridges and Westfield. I joined Westfield (now URW) five years ago on the Westfield Stratford City mall, which is on my doorstep and suits my lifestyle. It's a short commute, which means I can run to work. I am responsible for the creative delivery of a mall housing over 350 units, combining retail, dining, and leisure experiences. I have worked on many industry-award-winning projects, first to market and new concept design projects, with tenants including & Other Stories, Adidas, AllSaints, ARKET, Colicci, Hollister Co., Missguided, Morphe, and Zara. There are too many to list on this job!

A typical day

There is no typical day or week. Every day is different, which keeps it interesting. At any one time, I work on multiple tenancy projects with brands who lease units within Westfield Stratford City, from anchors to major retailers and independents over all sectors at macro to micro scale. My role is creative design management, which involves brand guardianship, creative direction of concept, and development into build. There are always a lot of meetings both scheduled and ad hoc, which are in the office, in the mall, and on construction sites, as well as international calls working across time zones. Communication and negotiating are key parts of my role. Challenging situations often arise, which requires quick thinking, problem-solving, providing design solutions, and decision-making, as well as teamwork often at a fast pace.

What do you love about being an interior designer?

I love working on real spaces that actually do get built. My degree in interior design has taken me on a great and unexpected journey at times but has shaped the designer I am today through my experience. Throughout my career I have worked internationally and travelled extensively around the world, which has broadened my horizons.

It is great to take a brand on a journey from blue sky concept to construction. Brand spaces are great platforms for experience and storytelling. Stores have to be so much more than 'rack and stack' stockrooms today. It is always very satisfying standing back on store opening day and seeing the results.

123

Be curious.

Lorna Mangan

Senior FF&E designer
David Collins Studio

124

Specialist in:
FF&E

Title of your degree:
BA (Hons)
Interior Design

Career overview

The search for my first design job really started a year before graduation. I won a competition for a hotel design concept, which led to my work being published by a hospitality design magazine. I was invited down to London to speak at a conference and attend an awards ceremony. I used this incredible opportunity to network, so when it came to apply for jobs, I had direct contact with directors who I'd met in person.

My career started immediately after graduation when I moved down to London to start working for Jestico + Whiles architects. I was offered a role as a junior designer within the interior department, which focused solely on hospitality projects, and it was there that I began to understand how a design studio operates and the stages of design develop. I worked closely with the interior design director and found myself enjoying the concept work, material selection, and furniture design much more than the space planning and drawing work. But I trained in all areas, which gave me an understanding as an all-round designer. We worked on some exciting projects, such as Hard Rock Hotel Ibiza and Aqua Shard.

Two years into my time in London I felt a need for a new challenge, and I was asked to join a small start-up company called Twenty2Degrees. This middleweight design opportunity gave me the chance to see a small studio grow and evolve. I was able to apply my skills learnt in my previous role and contribute to both the projects and the organization of the studio. During this time, the main project I worked on was Hilton Bankside in collaboration with Dexter Moren Associates. It was great visiting the site in London and seeing a hotel being built from its foundations. Although I was hired as an interior designer, I found again that I enjoyed the FF&E side much more than the technical drawing, and my responsibilities shifted towards this role as time went on.

My next career move took me to United Design Partnership, an interior design studio working on both hospitality and residential development projects. I joined as a senior designer and began working on the space planning for a development in London, but I soon found that I really didn't enjoy this design role and decided to speak to the CEO and express my wish to move on to the FF&E team, which he accepted. From this point I was able to really love my work again, and I thrived in this role, leading a small team and developing my management skills. In my time at United I worked with some amazing clients, such as W Hotels and Versace, and I travelled frequently, which has become a part of my job that I love.

I have always loved and admired the work of David Collins, so when an opportunity arose to join his studio, I felt it was something I could not pass. Although David sadly passed away a few years ago, his studio had continued to grow and evolve under his name, so this has been an exciting time to join the company. I've been able to work on some extremely prestigious projects, travelling internationally, and gaining a great deal of experience.

→

Lorna Mangan
portfolio excerpts

Hilton Bankside, London (2014) Public Areas
Twenty2Degrees & Dexter Moren Associates

This project was a joint venture with Dexter Moren Architects. We both worked closely with the Hilton brand managers and design director to bring together a concept that would push the boundaries of what is usually found in this corporate hotel group. Hilton Bankside is to be heralded as their new UK Flagship. We needed to present the future of the Hilton brand and it's progression into more stimulating designs and enriching environments. We drew inspiration from the sites proximity to the Tate Modern. Our interior reflects the urban landscape and London's history, with art playing an important role in it's ambience. I worked on the public areas from initial concept to detail design, which included drawing packages, specifications and bespoke furniture design. The hotel is now open and a popular destination in the newly developed area of Bankside.

My role in this project

- Selection of finishes
- Selection of FF&E & accessories
- Bespoke furniture design
- Liaising with art consultant
- Scheduling of finishes & FF&E
- Detail design stage drawing package
- Material boards for sign off
- Rendered plans & elevations
- Design Presentations
- Directing visualisers to produce CGIs

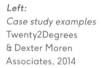

Left:
Case study examples
Twenty2Degrees
& Dexter Moren
Associates, 2014

WDoha, WHotel, Qatar (2017)
UNITED DESIGN PARTNERSHIP

WDoha are one of our long acquainted clients and since United designed the hotel ten years ago, I have been working on the gradual refurbishment over the last two years. We have recently refurbished the Market restaurant, the Wahm Bar & Wet Deck as well as the the Living Room, which will go on site later this year. I have been working alongside one of our other design directors to produce the concepts, material palettes and the FF&E packages. This fun and trendy hotel has continued to be a favourite destination amongst the locals, expatriates & visitors in Doha.

My role in this project

- Client meetings and presentations
- Selection of finishes
- Selection of FF&E & accessories
- Bespoke designed furniture
- Artwork concept
- Directing visualisers to produce CGIs
- Scheduling of finishes & FF&E
- Material boards for sign off
- Site visits

Left:
Case study examples
United Design
Partnership, 2017

126

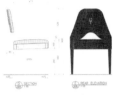

Aqua Shard Restaurant, David Yeo, London (2013)
JESTICO + WHILES

Located on the 31st floor of the tallest building in London, this unique restaurant offers quintessential British cuisine with an exceptional view. I worked closely with our Interior Design Director from concept stage, to design development, through to installation. I was largely involved in the FF+E and finishes specification, and the bespoke design of all of the furniture and chandeliers. This required developing the pieces from initial sketches, to liaising with furniture manufacturers, to detailing the designs, signing off samples and putting the order into production. I also worked with a London Taxidermy to create a beautiful butterfly display which I installed on site for the final touch.

My role in this project

- Selection of finishes
- Selection of FF&E & accessories
- Artwork concept & procurement
- Bespoke furniture design
- Bespoke lighting design
- Scheduling of finishes & FF&E
- Rendering plans & elevations
- Concept stage drawing package
- Material boards for sign off
- Site visits & snagging inspections

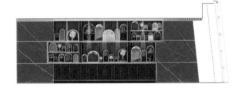

127

Residential Development, Moscow (2017)
UNITED DESIGN PARTNERSHIP

This luxurious residential development offers fifty grand apartments alongside excellent amenities, including a spa, gym, cigar room, salon, and children's study. The interiors merge classic and contemporary style with a nod to the Neo Classical Russian architecture. The underlying concept is inspired by a famous Russian geologist Vernadskiogo who the building is named after. It is interpreted through layering and mixing natural stone to create organic forms, set against traditional detailing. The beautifully crafted furniture has been carefully selected to compliment the interior design and suit the prestigious clientele. This project is on site and due for completion 2019.

My role in this project

- Selection of finishes
- Selection of FF&E & accessories
- Liaising with art consultant
- Bespoke lighting design
- Directing visualisers to produce CGIs
- Scheduling of finishes & FF&E
- Material boards for sign off
- Costing and budget management
- Client meetings & presentations

So far, I have seen the completion of Le Méridian Seoul, which I worked on the styling and shooting for, the refurbishment of Le Bar Américain in Monte-Carlo, followed by the opening of a new restaurant for the same client. I have also travelled to New York frequently to complete the anticipated TAK Room for chef Thomas Keller, along with many other projects.

A typical day

No day is the same! Depending on the stages of the projects I am working on, my day can involve anything from concept research, building material palettes, sketching furniture, preparing presentations, briefing visualizers, writing specifications, reviewing drawings, internal reviews, travelling, inspecting custom furniture and lighting, on-site snagging, installing furniture, and styling and shooting with incredible photographers.

What do you love about being an interior designer?

Getting to create incredible spaces for people to enjoy, and beyond that we can influence and inspire other creatives. There are not many jobs out there that combine creative thinking with technicality and attention to detail the way interior design does. It can be incredibly challenging, but every day I am grateful for being able to fuse my passion with a job that also allows the opportunity for travelling and collaborating with amazing artisans and interesting clients.

128

Don't be afraid to break boundaries.

129

Top left:
Solstice, Will Alsop and
Damsonetti Property Group, London
United Design Partnership, 2016

Top right:
Khalifa Tennis and Squash Complex,
stadium lounge, Doha
United Design Partnership, 2015-17

What advice would you give to interior designers starting out in their career?

Studios are bombarded with emails for job request daily, so if you want to be noticed, you need to be unique and bold in your approach. When applying for my first job, I sent out small cards that looked like beautifully wrapped invitations, and inside they had a snippet of my portfolio and my contact.

Be confident and committed to your ideas and don't be afraid to break boundaries.

Ask questions and be curious. Learn from your senior designer and directors – skills and knowledge often come with experience.

Get out there and see things! It's the best way to find inspiration and the only way to really understand what works and what doesn't. Go and sit at the bar or sneak a look in the hotel spa. The more you are analysing your surroundings, the easier it will become to apply that knowledge to your designs.

Martha Gray

Middleweight interior designer
BDG Architecture + Design

Specialist in:

Workplace, mixed-use, and commercial

Title of your degree:

BA (Hons) Interior Architecture

Career overview

My fascination with architecture and design began at an early age. I found buildings to be such honest and alive representations of times that have past as well as suggestions of future. With this in mind, I did some summer work experience for Jackson-Stops & Staff estate agents when I was sixteen in order to explore my interest in buildings. I soon realized that I was more interested in designing spaces than selling them, which then propelled me into hunting for another summer internship when I was eighteen. That summer I interned with TH2 (residential) and had a great insight into the finishing of high-end residences in London. The summer after my second year at university, I secured another internship with construction services global giant AECOM. Once finished with my studies at Northumbria, AECOM offered me a job as a graduate designer. I worked on a range of medium- to very-large-scale workplace projects in big and highly skilled teams. I worked hard

for two years and eventually left the company after completion of the graduate scheme in order to move to Australia in pursuit of adventure. I interviewed with approximately twenty companies across Sydney and Melbourne and received two job offers: one from Futurespace and one from Siren Design Group, as well as rumblings of potential offers from other companies in the pipeline too. While both formal offers were very strong options, I decided to work for Siren due to the reception I'd received and atmosphere I'd felt so inspired by, not to mention the very cool clients and projects. I was given the title of interior designer and a sponsored visa to remain in the country. While at Siren, I worked across an array of workplace (predominantly), hospitality, mixed use, commercial, and retail projects of all sizes. I have now recently returned to London (after nearly two years in Australia) and have recently started working for BDG Architecture + Design as a middleweight interior designer.

→

Martha Gray
portfolio excerpts

Image: Hufton+Crow

Left:
AECOM EMEA+I HQ,
London
AECOM, Strategy Plus,
2017

Left:
Uber, Sydney
Siren Design Group,
2018

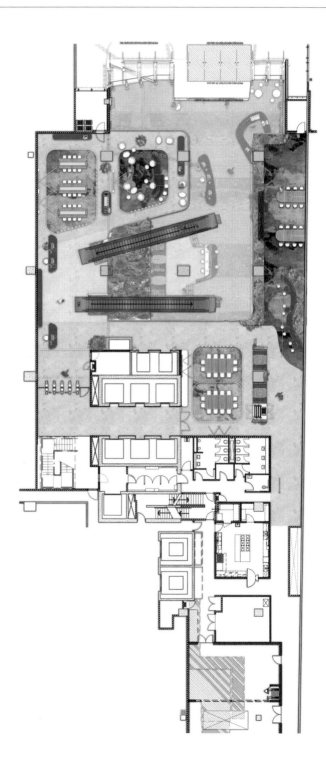

133

Right:
Charterhall, Raine Square, Perth
Siren Design Group, 2020

A typical day

I'm working pretty heavily on SketchUp and InDesign at the moment for our stage three deadline for a workplace project due in a couple of weeks. Although, the past three days I have been on internal Revit training, which has been great.

What do you love about being an interior designer?

Being able to physically see the end result of all of your hard work and impacting the everyday lives of people, as well as getting the opportunity to work with companies and gain an understanding around who they are and how they want to attract and retain staff.

134

Right:
Hall & Wilcox offices, Sydney
Siren Design Group, 2020

Don't <u>overwork</u> your projects when it's unnecessary

What advice would you give to interior designers starting out in their career?

Take advice when people offer it, and always say yes to a coffee.

Grab any internships you can – a lot of companies don't hire graduates without internship experience first.

Make friends in the industry who can give you non-biased(ish) advice on the market, i.e. suppliers, recruiters, strategists, engineers, etc. Go to the industry parties!

Don't overwork your projects when it's unnecessary – consider what the fee is for the job and allow that to inform the work you're producing.

Up-skill yourself. Make sure you're on top of at least three of the five basic programs it's necessary to know (InDesign, AutoCAD, Photoshop, Revit, SketchUp).

135

Matthew Davies

Head of interior design
Ambassador Theatre Group

136

Specialist in:

Bar and restaurant, hospitality, and retail

Title of your degree:

BA (Hons) Interior Design

Career overview

After studying at the Surrey Institute, I started my career in retail design at Brinkworth, having completed a work experience placement during the third year of my degree. This led to a full-time job after I graduated, working on high-street stores such as AllSaints and Karen Millen. This was a great first opportunity to be involved in some quick turn over and pretty creative projects, in a really sociable working environment.

After three years, (and following the recession in 2008) the opportunity arose to be able to move across into bars and restaurants at Dover Design, where the industry was surviving a little better than retail. This gave me the opportunity to grow and hone my skill set, gaining more responsibility and managing key clients at the time such as Zizzi. Being trusted with the client-facing aspect of a project at this early stage of my career really helped to progress me into a more senior role, where I started to oversee junior designers through the design stages and focus more on the delivery/site management side of a project.

Following travels in 2014, I returned and took the opportunity to integrate myself back into the industry through some freelance work at 20.20, which included working on the Liverpool Football Club Anfield Stadium expansion. This had the added benefit of a move into hospitality, which essentially added an extra string to my bow, and was one I immediately benefitted from when offered a role as senior designer at Virgin Atlantic. This was obviously a move to an in-house role and not something I took lightly, as I think there can be a general perception this moves you away from the creative side of the role and more towards management. In a sense this can be true, but the role at Virgin Atlantic gave me the chance to manage and lead external design companies to deliver the new Upper Class Clubhouse at Gatwick. This brought about more experience in managing large-scale projects and was the largest budget I had managed to date.

→

Matthew Davies
portfolio excerpts

138

Left:
Virgin Atlantic
Upper Class
Clubhouse, Gatwick
Virgin Atlantic
in-house studio, 2017

Left:
Zizzi restaurant
interior, Metrocentre
Dover Design, 2010

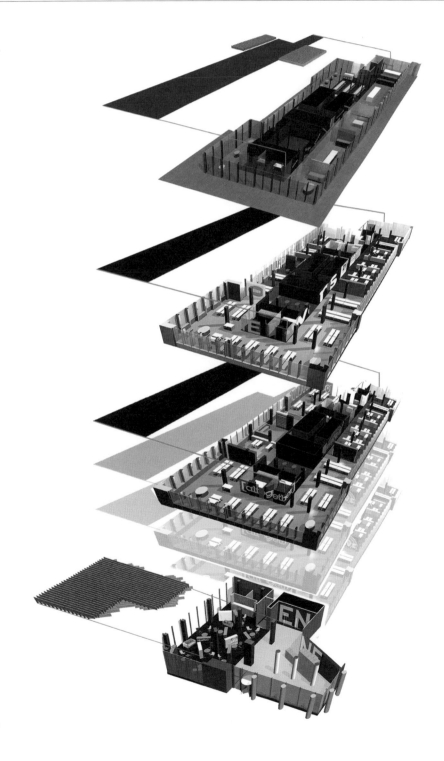

Right:
Office pitch
Brinkworth, 2008

I always like to think I would take roles I find interesting, irrespective of other factors sometimes considered more important by others. This is something that was demonstrated when the role at Ambassador Theatre Group presented itself.

I joined in October 2017 as the head of interior design and in less than two years have grown the team to four, delivering projects across our London, UK, and US portfolio of theatres, from Torquay to Texas, Edinburgh to Boston. The buildings themselves could be considered living, breathing beings, so the chance to use my acquired expertise in retail, bar, restaurant, and hospitality in, for example, a 220-year-old Grade II listed building was too good to turn down and something I'm relishing.

A typical day

My company owns fifty theatres across the UK, Germany, and the US, so our small in-house team can involve projects such as (but not limited to) bar refurbishments, lounge fitouts, snack and merchandise kiosk roll-outs, toilet refurbishments, dressing room refurbishments, and in some instances the auditoriums themselves.

What do you love about being an interior designer?

The main thing I've always loved about my role, is the ability to create spaces that people can and want to use. Being able to oversee the entire process, from a sketch on a piece of scrap paper to the real thing in front of you, is hugely rewarding and something I'll never get bored of.

What advice would you give to interior designers starting out in their career?

Take the jobs you find interesting. There's no single way to go about developing and growing within this industry, so if you have a chance to do something different but interesting, take it. I'm really proud of the fact that I've enjoyed all of the roles I've taken.

141

Left:
Concept sketch for retail pitch
Brinkworth, 2009

Above:
Apollo Victoria theatre kiosk
Ambassador Theatre Group, 2018

Nick Gierus

Senior 3D designer
Jack Morton Worldwide

Specialist in:

Exhibitions, events,
and retail

Title of your degrees:

MA Design Futures
BA (Hons) Industrial Design

Career overview

Like most students, I earnt a little extra cash as a barman during my studies. This continued into the first six months after graduation until I got my break working for a graphics and multimedia company in Germany, drawing cars and products for the automotive industry. I was recommended by an ex fellow student and went out for a week's trial. I'd done just enough to convince the company to keep me on. It was a very close decision. I was nervous, wanted it very badly, and had next to no confidence at the time. It taught me two things: how to work fast and how to work intelligently (re-use what you've created whenever possible, whenever appropriate). We worked for companies like Vauxhall and Porsche. My dirty little secret when I was out there was that I'm no car freak. I did, however, still enjoy the process of creating designs and producing visuals.

After this I did a master's degree in London, which is one of the best things I've ever done. It allowed me to explore the subject of design much more deeply. My first degree was all about how best to put another product on the shelves for people to buy. The master's taught me how to consider designs from a more socio-economic and sustainable point of view. I got to meet some cracking people, be a student all over again (which was brilliant), and had the most wonderful lecturer who seemed to be composed of equal parts philosopher, musician, artist, and counsellor – think a cross between Stephen Fry and Bowie. My dissertation was about the re-humanizing effects of interactive street furniture in public spaces. Here I learned the importance of designing, not simply a product but a process. When you design a process (a desired outcome or a system), the required tool for making that outcome happen can often reveal itself.

Soon after graduation I managed to score a job as a 3D designer at an architects firm designing furniture and products. I drifted into the actual architectural work very heavily just by simply being in the studio and offering my services as a space planner and draftsperson. I did this purely to stick around.

$\longrightarrow$

Nick Gierus
portfolio excerpts

144

Left:
Abu Dhabi
International Airport
F&B experience
Portland Design, 2015

Left:
Goodwood Festival
of Speed, Ford
Jack Morton, 2019

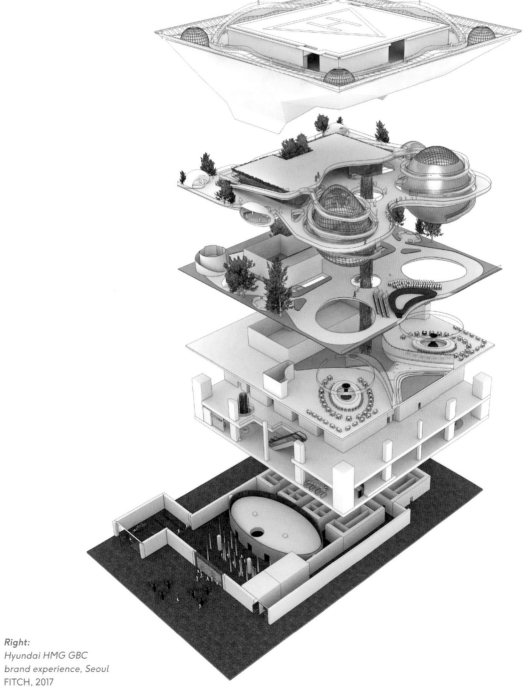

Right:
Hyundai HMG GBC
brand experience, Seoul
FITCH, 2017

Everyone gets a bit frightened in their career – don't let it consume you.

146

I was freelance with them and the product work was limited. By using my existing design skills and diversifying, I quickly became very useful. I also discovered that I absolutely loved spaces as much as products. I stayed for four years.

For me, products and spaces equalled exhibition design, and this is where I've landed in my career to date. Seven years ago, I took the decision to become freelance again, and it turned out to be perfect timing for how I wanted to work and develop. I've been lucky enough to work at some incredible agencies, like Imagination, FITCH, and now Jack Morton. I've also been involved in some great projects for Jaguar Land Rover, Cartoon Network, Samsung, and Google. I make plenty of mistakes, but I always worked hard, am generous with my support to my colleagues, try to be honest as often as I can and – massively important to me this one – I always, always try to develop and be better. Design yourself too – that's what I say.

A typical day

The teams that I work with explore a brand, discover and create its stories, and finally design a space or event to support these stories. I contribute to this process and then ultimately visualize everything in 3D (images and animations). I also create production drawings of how the various components are to be built.

What do you love about being an interior designer?

Having ideas. When you start a project, it's in a state of pure potential. It literally can be anything. I read once that one of humanity's most intimidating challenges has been how best to engage with a blank piece of paper. Which is equally exciting and terrifying?

All of that is worth it, though, just to get to that moment of having what you believe to be a 'good idea'. Good ideas are quite the rush.

What advice would you give to interior designers starting out in their career?

Accept that everyone gets a bit frightened in their career and spends more time than they need doubting themselves, too. So don't allow those feelings to consume you when they decide to pop in for a visit.

Share all that you've learned – it comes back tenfold.

There isn't a single perfect all-rounder designer out there. Try to always be as up front as possible with what you can achieve. And don't feel bad about what you can't.

Try to enjoy all of this. We're dealing with telling stories, creating wonderfully enriching spaces, and making memorable environments. We're very lucky to have discovered the sheer amazingness of design this early on in our lives.

147

Right:
Jaguar Land Rover,
Paris Motor Show
Imagination, 2012

Paul Digby

Creative director
HMKM

Specialist in:
Retail

Title of your degree:
BA (Hons)
Interior Design

Career overview

After graduating from Manchester University, I moved to London and began looking for a job at a design consultancy, calling agencies and trying to get my foot in the door at every opportunity. Aside from talking with recruiters, I'd write letters to designers and be on the phone asking to meet them even if a position wasn't available. After any meeting I'd ask the designer for advice or if they had any other contacts to approach within the industry. Always leaving with a 'next step' to pursue, I managed to get my first role in design through this process.

During my early years, I found it very useful to look at all aspects of project delivery to ensure I continued my understanding of how you practise interior design. From concept sketching, detailing, and being on site, I found approaching each challenge in my first few years with enthusiasm allowed the next one to feel like real career progress.

Once I'd spent a few years as a junior interior designer with a handful of consultancies, I pursued a role as a middleweight at David Collins Studio. They had a series of luxury retail projects outside of their usual hospitality mainstay, so I joined their expanding design team. From Amanda Wakeley and her fashion store to David Morris, 'The London Jeweller', I got a lot of experience understanding detail and materiality, given the premium nature of the clients. Often I would find myself running the projects, which was great experience – daunting but rewarding in equal measure. Presenting to clients or attending meetings on my own, it was a steep learning curve.

While at David Collins Studio I began working on hospitality and residential projects, which I realized weren't what I ultimately enjoyed or wanted to progress my career in. I decided I needed a change. Realizing my interest in retail work, I joined Din Associates, where I worked on their Harrods projects.

→

Paul Digby
portfolio excerpts

150

Left:
Finished concept store
for Country Road,
Chadstone Mall,
Melbourne
HMKM, 2019

Left:
Pewter room sketch,
Svenskt Tenn,
Stockholm
HMKM, 2011

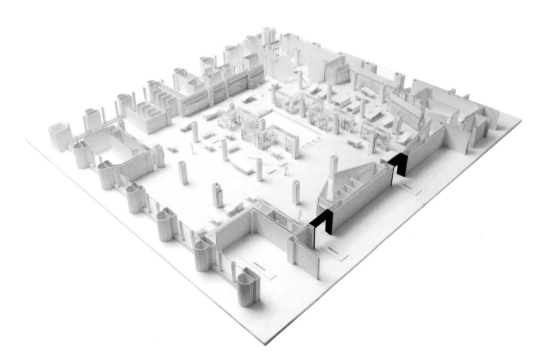

Top and right:
Working model and
finished space,
Denim Studio,
Selfridges, London
HMKM, 2015

Image: Marcus Peel

How you present yourself is as important as the content of your work.

152

My experience with luxury design was immediately transferrable to help with the concepts. I learnt a lot during my time there, understanding the deeper skills needed within the retail sector having come from somewhere quite different in design approach and aesthetic. Adjusting from one sector to another can be quite difficult in later years as the expectation is higher, so it's important to try different consultancies and projects to find the right fit and to broaden your experience.

Having built a more differentiated portfolio (tailored for each specific interview) and diversified skill set, I applied for a job at HMKM where I still am today. They saw a more cohesive body of work in premium fashion retail in my folio, after the combined experience gained at my previous practices. HMKM place a strong emphasis on creative output being collaborative with strong detailing and narrative. Having started as a senior designer, initially responsible for the Selfridges projects, I worked my way up to the role of creative director, managing a variety of international projects that go through the studio.

HMKM was subsequently bought by Interbrand, the strategy and branding group. Working alongside them has brought with it opportunities to broaden our sector reach, expanding the business to work with Interbrand's clients and projects — a new and exciting challenge in an ever-evolving industry.

A typical day

I'm involved in ensuring that each project's creative output aligns with the expectation of the client. Each project is different, but the end result should always be the same: a client who is happy with the finished project and satisfied with how we worked together to achieve the final scheme. Equally, my role is to ensure my team are pleased with their work. Our industry can be very frustrating, so I work hard to create an environment where creativity can thrive.

What do you love about being an interior designer?

The variety of the work I do is what I love most about being an interior designer. Project scales vary, each brief is different, and I get to work with a vast variety of people. The opportunity to create something new and inspiring ensures it's a new challenge every day.

What advice would you give to interior designers starting out in their career?

For an interior designer starting out it's important when interviewing to present the best work you have done so far. You won't be expected to have immediately transferrable skills after graduating unless you've done a placement or have had work experience. In addition, how you present yourself is as important as the content of your work. The design landscape is changing, so having a point of view on topics such as sustainability and inclusivity is becoming as important as the actual design. We always look for someone who will align with our values and work culture, someone who is eager to learn and will enjoy being part of our team.

Pernille Lind

Designer and director
Pernille Lind Studio *and* **LIND + ALMOND**

Specialist in:
Interior design
and furniture design

Title of your degrees:
MA Spatial Design
BA (Hons) Interior Design

Career overview

I received my MA in 2010 and started my first job as an interior designer in a small Danish company called Design By Us. My role was very diverse and exciting as there were only four team members in the company. After a couple of years working there, I realized that the company and general industry (mainly for interior designers) in Denmark was quite small and I wanted to work on bigger international projects. Therefore, I decided to move back to London. To get into the London market as a 'foreign-based' designer was quite difficult, so I ended up taking a three-month intern role at Tom Dixon's Design Research Studio, which lead to an offer as a freelancer. However, by this time I had already been given a full-time role as an interior designer at Anouska Hempel Design. After spending a little over half a year at AHD, I then moved on to Conran and Partners. This was a great move for me as the team was quite small at the time, meaning I was given the opportunity to take on a lot of responsibility and had creative freedom. I was given more leading roles on big projects, including hotels, restaurants, and high-end residentials, and in line with the team growing, my role also grew. However, after some years the company went in a direction which I was not totally comfortable with from a project-based perspective, and out of the blue I was asked by Soho House & Co. to apply for a role as the senior designer in their growing design department. I thought it was a very interesting move to go 'client side'. This was also at a point where Soho House's expansion plans were in full flourish, so they needed designers to grow their internal team. Again, I found myself in a 'small' team

compared to the amount of work which needed to be done, and this was a great challenge and learning curve. I was leading the development and creative direction of their co-working space, Soho Works, in Shoreditch, which included sites in Istanbul and LA (at the time). My role at Soho House gave me valuable insight into the workings of a growing brand and international operator. I was given autonomy and responsibility, which could in some respects be compared to the tasks you would have to be covering if you were running your own business.

While working at Soho House, I was contacted by someone who became my client for Hotel Sanders. He was looking for a designer with international experience to take on the leading role in developing the interior design and brand identity for Copenhagen's first boutique hotel.

$\longrightarrow$

Pernille Lind
portfolio excerpts

Left:
Guest room, Hotel Sanders, Copenhagen
Pernille Lind Studio, 2017

Left:
Living room fireplace, Long Residence
Pernille Lind Studio, 2019

Right:
The Lake Townhouse,
Copenhagen
Pernille Lind Studio,
2018

Above:
Long Residence
Pernille Lind Studio, 2019

158

If you need a new challenge or a change, speak up.

This was a chance I couldn't say no to. I quickly realized that it was going to be a mammoth task so asked my partner Richy Almond if he would take on the project with me. Luckily, he said yes, and we formed our first company together LIND + ALMOND in 2015. After two and a half years of non-stop work, passion, and dedication, Hotel Sanders opened in winter 2017 and has been a huge success both locally and with world travellers, and has even won a couple of awards. After completing the project, I needed to take a break and reassess what kind of work/life balance I wanted. I decided to start my own company in order to take on smaller residential and commercial projects, which I have been running since the beginning of 2018.

A typical day

I've just come back from a final install trip for a residential project I've been working on in Chicago. I have very varied weeks, as I work on three to five projects at a time, all in different stages and countries. I have a couple of freelancers who help me out at times when the workload is especially high. Otherwise I do most of the work myself, from concepts, CAD drawings, meeting with suppliers/manufacturers, and general project and client management.

What do you love about being an interior designer?

Design is my passion, not just interior design but all design. Being an interior designer means you get the chance to work across many forms of design disciplines, and the creatives behind these become part of your greater team. I have the opportunity to understand and explore how furniture, ceramics, lighting, fabrics, photography, art, and other specialist craft and artisan work is being developed and handed down from previous generations. Consequently, I get a holistic understanding of how to create a scheme that pays tribute to all the wonderful furniture designs, objects, art, and textural layers that make up a personal and enchanting interior experience. Furthermore, I work with specialists in creating my own designs, which also forms part of every project I do.

What advice would you give to interior designers starting out in their career?

When you are a junior, find a senior who has the interest and time to mentor you, and always ask questions about anything you are in doubt of.

If you need a new challenge or a change, speak up and communicate this constructively with your managers or directors.

Be prepared for the future. Take steps in the present to acquire and practise the skills you'll need to make that jump.

Experience is key and this takes time, so be patient towards yourself alongside pushing your own growth and talent.

Right:
The Lake Townhouse,
Copenhagen
Pernille Lind Studio,
2018

159

Roland Hartmann

Managing director
Hartmann Designs

Specialist in:
Residential, commercial,
and hospitality

Title of your degree:
Higher National Diploma in
Interior Design

Career overview

It was always in the stars that I was to be an interior designer. I grew up in South Africa in a furniture-manufacturing family, and from a young age I remember always re-designing my bedroom and working in the factory during my school holidays. After completing school I did the obligatory national service, travelled Europe, and attended courses in fine art and graphic design. Through a friend I was introduced to an interior designer who offered me a part-time job as a junior designer/runner. I knew immediately that I had found my vocation and proceeded to study interior design and at the same time continued to work in design practices on a part-time basis. I also ran a small but successful paint finish company to supplement my income. At the time this was all the rage.

After completing my course, I decided to move to the UK and pursue my career in interior design. It was fortuitous that I had a contact at a well-known hospitality design company, which I joined at a junior/intern level and worked myself up to a senior designer position. I must add that I only secured this position by volunteering myself as an intern with a minimal income. I held a second job at Heals as a salesperson to support myself. During my time in this practice I was exposed to all areas of design, from preparing specification schedules, drawing packages, specifying FF&E, preparing full concept presentations (very tiring and demanding as there is always a deadline), and finally site work. The majority of the projects were international hotel groups, and this exposure and experience opened an opportunity to work abroad. I then proceeded to work on a large Luxury Collection Sheraton Hotel in Addis Ababa, Ethiopia for four years.

Following this assignment, I returned to London and set up a studio for an American design practice and worked on both high-end residential and hospitality projects for two years. It was during this time that I decided to venture out on my own and have since been running a small but successful practice specializing in high-end residential projects, specifically apartments. I do work for both private individuals, contractors, and developers. If I look back over the years, I see a pattern that clearly shows I have always been independent and a leader, and even though I have managed my own company for the last ten or so years, the sum of my success and achievements is down to my team members and every single person working on the projects, not to mention the clients for giving us the opportunities.

Roland Hartmann
portfolio excerpts

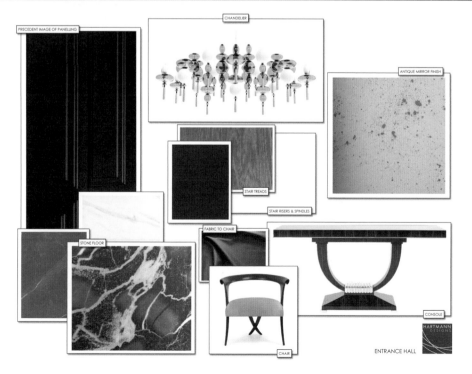

162

CHANDELIER

ANTIQUE MIRROR FINISH

STAIR TREADS

STAIR RISERS & SPINDLES

STONE FLOOR

FABRIC TO CHAIR

CHAIR

CONSOLE

HARTMANN
DESIGNS

ENTRANCE HALL

Top and left:
Sheldon Avenue
entrance hall
Hartmann Designs,
2019

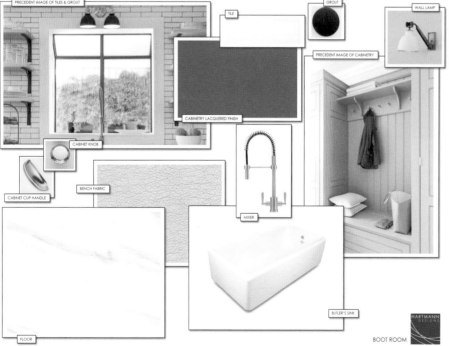

Top and right:
Sheldon Avenue
boot room
Hartmann Designs,
2019

A typical day

I am an early riser and use this time to run through all my emails before the day starts. I respond to most queries that were not dealt with the day before and file relevant emails. A typical day will consist of design team meetings, site visits, client meetings, and lots and lots of administration. Being an interior designer requires you not only to do the creative stuff but to be able to do the administrative work too. I have been told this job is 97% hard work and 3% creativity, and I believe it to be true. It is crucial as a designer to be organized and to plan your days, weeks, and months in advance. This can be done by simply creating a week/month/year calendar: calendarpedia.co.uk

What do you love about being an interior designer?

The amazing people you meet on the way, the wonderful places you get to visit, and the exciting and challenging projects you get to work on. And to add to this, the wonderful part of being a designer is that no day is the same. One day it can be office-based, the next on site, or another meeting with clients, or travelling abroad. And it is truly a profession that every single day you are exposed to new information and situations that ultimately allows one to become a competent, confident, and unique designer.

This job is 97% hard work and 3% creativity.

What advice would you give to interior designers starting out in their career?

You need to love this profession and understand as previously stated it is not all glamorous. It is a lot of hard work, more often with very little recognition. It is a profession that requires absolute commitment, resolve, patience, persistence, and above all observation of our environment and the world around us. I do not want to sound clichéd, but it is our responsibility to make this world a better place by improving the built environment and importantly being conscious of what footprint we leave behind. This is quite difficult to achieve in luxury design but slowly opportunities are arising with manufacturers and suppliers. Beauty or uniqueness will glow when it is obvious that there is attention to detail and consideration given to the design.

165

Left and top:
Roland's sketches

Roselind Wilson

Owner and creative director
Roselind Wilson Design Ltd

Specialist in:

Residential

Title of your degree:

BCom (Bachelor of Commerce)
in Business Management and
Diploma in Interior Design

Career overview

Although I had always wanted to be an interior designer, I wasn't able to study this directly after leaving school. Instead I started working (two jobs in fact) to support myself and save for my future studies. In the interim I worked very hard at the jobs I was in to ensure I could learn as much as possible about working with people and managing my time and task load. When I was able, I commenced with my studies to acquire my degree, which I studied for part time to ensure I could still maintain my permanent job to pay bills, etc. It was towards the end of my degree that I started my interior design diploma, and given that I was working full time and completing the degree, I had to be extremely diligent with my time to ensure I could manage the workload. What it did teach me was exactly that — to produce high-quality work while working diligently with limited time and resources.

When I graduated, I sought freelance work in the interior design industry and was also happy to obtain work experience, which I did at a few independent retail and design stores where I lived in Cape Town. I then applied for an interior designer position by proactively contacting a designer whose work I really liked, and my initiative and persistence paid off. I worked at this company until I relocated to the UK in 2005. I was extremely grateful for the experience I gained there as I was the owner's right-hand person, and although it was a 'baptism of fire', I learned and was fully involved in every aspect of the design process. When I relocated to the UK, I was very specific and strategic about my career. And I mention this with earnest as it was always my dream to have my own studio. So I carefully researched design companies I would like to work for and ended up with a shortlist of my top three companies.

$\longrightarrow$

Roselind Wilson
portfolio excerpts

Image: Richard Waite

Left:
*The Bromptons
master bathroom*
Roselind Wilson
Design Ltd, 2014

*Left:
The Bromptons
sitting room*
Roselind Wilson
Design Ltd, 2014

Right:
Carlton Hill
entrance hall
Roselind Wilson
Design Ltd, 2018

Image: Mel Yates

170

When I arrived in the UK,
I was offered a job as a kitchen
designer at Smallbone but
rejected this offer given I had
experience of the full project
process and did not want to be
too niche in my experience.
I was glad I waited, as a few
weeks later I was offered a
position as an interior designer
at a small property development
company. This opened up a
wealth of experience for me as I
single-handedly managed their
small refurb projects but also
worked alongside the architect
on larger refurbishment projects.
A year into this I felt ready to
apply to my top choice of firm:
Helen Green Design. I bit the
bullet, sent in my CV, and got
the job. And that set me well
on my path to self-employment
as I worked my way up from
interior designer to senior design
manager, working on some of
the most prestigious interior
design projects in London.

A typical day

I have a wonderful design team and I am also fortunate enough to have my twin sister work alongside me in running the business. So right now my day is spent meeting with my team to review project designs and details, and ensure that everything is running seamlessly and that any concerns are dealt with as a team as quickly as possible.

My sister is the CMO, and she meets with me to review marketing initiatives and planning of the marketing budgets. Together we review the project forecasting and jobs profitability.

My most important aspect of any day would be to ensure all our clients are completely happy and satisfied, and I speak with them regularly as the relationships we build and nurture with them are the key to the longevity of the company.

What do you love about being an interior designer?

For me, I thrive on the fact that I get to meet and design the homes for our diverse clientele. Our clients are windows to the world, and through them we get to experience a range and diversity of tastes and cultures. We have clients from all over the world, and it is an absolute honour to be able to design such an intimate space as their home.

What advice would you give to interior designers starting out in their career?

This is a challenging industry with low barriers to entry, so at any point in time there is a lot of competition. You need to develop your skills and focus on standing out – be authentic and individual and determined, and with that attitude you will be surprised how far you can go.

Never make assumptions – what we do is factual, and assumptions can have a high cost. Always respect your client and yourself. To run a successful project, try and think as many steps ahead as possible. Develop a 'we' attitude and not an 'I' attitude, as many hands make light work and many heads can solve a problem. Don't take it all on alone – there are far too many tasks and people to coordinate, and you are only human. It can be stressful and often is, but the end of each project is extremely satisfying.

171

Develop a 'we' attitude and not an 'I' attitude.

Suzy Huntley

Freelance senior designer
Suzy Huntley Freelance

172

Specialist in:
Retail, beauty, and
food and beverage

Title of your degree:
BA (Hons)
Interior Architecture
and Design

Career overview

After graduating in 2002, I returned to Checkland Kindleysides, securing a position as a junior designer as a result of my placement year with the company while at university. My placement year gave me invaluable experience that allowed me to grow in confidence as a designer and understand the differences between design at university and the reality of work in a 'real' studio. I spent four years working on large retail accounts, such as Boots, Levi's and Virgin Music. However, I felt restricted by this role the company had determined for me and decided that if I was going to become a 'fully rounded' designer then I would need to move to a different type of studio. I felt a smaller agency would offer greater opportunities and expose me to the full design process.

In 2006, I moved to Caulder Moore as a middleweight designer. At that point I had no idea that I would be at this company for twelve years and progress to design director! I'm often asked why I stayed so long,

and the answer is simple: the client list was amazing and exposed me to high-end retail, entrepreneurial brands and household names, as well as fantastic people. Some of which are now friends for life.

Being a small company, I was exposed to all aspects of design, from the initial vision and concept through to the practicalities of delivering the job on site for the client. I have worked on some amazing accounts throughout my career at Caulder Moore, taking Sweaty Betty from their first stand-alone store in London to international stores in the US and more recently their experiential flagship in Covent Garden. I got to travel internationally with brands such as Gina Shoes and reinvent household names such as New Look. I was also exposed to other sectors of design, delivering flagship hair salons for Trevor Sorbie both in the UK and internationally, as well as Fuller's first airport pub! I was involved in everything from pitching the initial vision to realizing the design on site. I have no idea where the twelve years went!

→

Suzy Huntley
portfolio excerpts

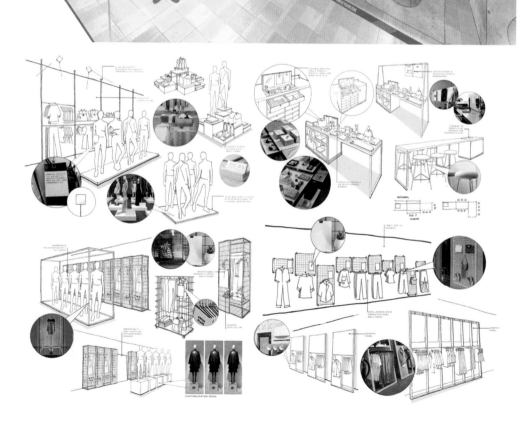

Top and left:
Sweaty Betty flagship
store concept,
Carnaby Street, London
Caulder Moore, 2017

175

Above:
Trevor Sorbie hair salon
concept mood boards
Caulder Moore, 2017

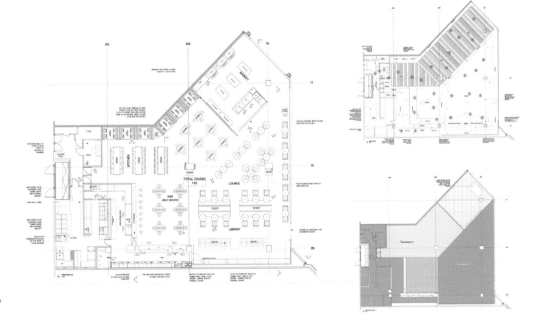

Right:
Fuller's, Heathrow T2
detail dwgs
Caulder Moore, 2013

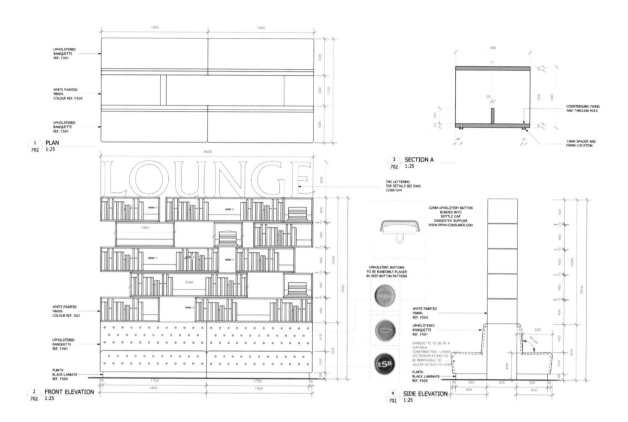

However, after working non-stop for a fast-paced agency for many years, I decided in 2019 I wanted to try something different, and with my second child on the way I needed to re-address my work/life balance. I decided to explore the option of freelancing. I knew this would mean a change in mind-set, as I would no longer be in control of projects from beginning to end and would have to be completely flexible to work on different projects in all different types of studios.

A typical day

Every new contract as a freelance designer is different. You can be entering a project at any stage and have to be completely flexible and adaptable to enable your client to get the best results. However, the first day is always key. You must absorb all information possible to enable you to get moving, be adaptable, and learn quickly how the company works. And never be afraid to ask questions. I have worked on everything from large supermarket projects to small concessions for an international toy store. Working on drawing packs one day to visualizing the next!

What do you love about being an interior designer?

What I have always loved about design is the reality of creating something on paper, realizing that vision, and then walking into the finished environment, knowing you have been part of that journey.

Far left:
Technical drawing

177

What advice would you give to interior designers starting out in their career?

Don't be defined by your degree result. When I was offered my placement year at Checkland Kindleysides, I asked 'Why me?' as I was against stronger candidates on paper. They told me I was chosen because I was passionate and talked about my work with enthusiasm. Communication skills are key in design, and how you present yourself goes a long way.

Design is a small world. Build relationships and networks as you never know who you will bump into along the way! People are key in design, and you can learn so much from all of them.

Don't ever regret your decisions or be afraid of taking a leap into the unknown. Everything I've done as a designer has shaped who I am today, and I look back over the work I have completed and am proud of every decision I made.

Design is a small world.

Tola Ojuolape

Senior project designer
Selina

Specialist in:

Hospitality and commercial

Title of your degrees:

MA Graphic Communication and Design

BA (Hons) Interior Architecture

Career overview

I graduated during the recession and couldn't get a job straight away at home in Ireland. I eventually secured an unpaid internship and decided to move to London after one and a half years to pursue my career and study further to stand me in good stead for securing a role. I was very nervous and had reached out to a few recruiters. Lucy [Painter] was one of the first people I reached out to prior to coming to the UK, and I touched base with her upon moving to London. I got a job through Lucy at Shopworks, a small firm in Berkhamsted, and did concepts in retail for them. The projects were all in global commercial retail. It was good experience that allowed me to work on a range of retail concepts in Russia, China, New York, and India.

After Shopworks, I worked at another practice and quickly realized it wasn't for me. It appeared to be the dream job as it allowed me to combine my background in interiors and branding; however, the projects and scale of the office just weren't the right fit. I realized I function better in a small-scale company where I can be mentored and learn more.

I chose to pivot to FF&E after freelancing at another company. My experience working at FF&E cemented my passion for design and allowed me to learn through a very different lens. It also enabled me to build a great network of suppliers, and I gained a lot of knowledge of materials, and sourcing and procurement of projects. I also got to travel a lot and worked on a diverse number of projects in the UK, Ghana, South Korea, Kazakhstan, and elsewhere.

This time also allowed me to evaluate my strengths and weaknesses. I knew I wanted to continue working in design full time. I chose to move into a corporate practice as I had spent time in cool, trendy design practices and learned so much. All of my experience, I believe, has set me up to work for an in-house brand where I can use the skills I've acquired, working with a diverse range of people across brand, procurement, and experience design, as I have essentially done a bit of it all. It also means I have had a broad range of experience on different projects, including commercial hospitality, workplaces, and a small number of residential projects.

→

Tola Ojuolape
portfolio excerpts

Concept Recap
Serebryanicheskaya's Craftsmanship District

17 | TITUL
Centr Invest
Interim Concept
July 2019

During a construction project on the Serebryanicheskaya Embankment, archaeologists found bits of two wooden houses dating back to the 17th or 18th century. It was a district of windmills, breweries, factories and paint shops. The district became prolific for Makers with various Metal Crafters including Minting, Metal Making, Metal Smelting & Die Casting.

Weaving Factory   Metal Engraving   Die Casting   Timber Carving

Condor | Residential House 2
Features & Characteristics - Softness

33 | TITUL
Centr Invest
Interim Concept
July 2019

We are inspired by the softness and contrast of the Condors features especially on the head of the Condor. The textured white covering can be translated in soft fabrics, and lightness in the interior space.

   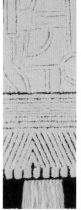 

Condor's Soft Feathers   Softness & Cosiness of Velvet Softness of Condor Collor   Lightness of Condor's White Collar

*Top and left:
Moodboards
AEDAF, 2019*

180

Right:
Bents sketches
FITCH, 2014

University and the working world are completely different.

A typical day

As I'm working in-house for a brand, a typical week involves a number of meetings with the head of development and the project manager assigned to my project. My project is in Brighton and is currently in the design development phase. Most of my time is spent developing the project through planning, sketches, 3D designs on SketchUp, and rendering in Photoshop. I also have to prepare a presentation for the wider team every week and spend some time sourcing and researching materials, finishes, and furniture. There is an upcycling element to the brand pillars at Selina, so we spend time coming up with ideas and sourcing items that can be made by our workshop and FF&E manager. We also visit the site quite often as the project is just an hour outside our offices in London.

What do you love about being an interior designer?

I love seeing a concept come alive – how it allows you to beautify a space and work with diverse skill sets to make it a reality. One of the best parts of what we do is also travelling to different places I may not have visited otherwise. I enjoy sourcing materials and learning about different types of craftsmanship, and I love how interior design enables me to converse with colour, pair materials, and bridges the lines between art, furniture, and product design.

182

Below:
Retail concept for The Coast Inn,
Skerries, Dublin
John Duffy Design Group, 2012

What advice would you give to interior designers starting out in their career?

Harness the basic skills and computer programs required to work in an office environment, such as AutoCAD, Vectorworks, and Adobe software. University and the working world are completely different, and computer programs will be required.

Understand your strengths and weaknesses and have a strategy for how to use them as there are many different types of design firms out there. If you are a very technical designer, you may struggle at a concept-led firm and vice versa.

As a young designer, you will work with people for a number of years until you work on your own projects, so find a mentor. It's important you have people to check in with and can be accountable to should there be any challenges along the way.

Find ways to always harness your creativity by looking outside interior design for inspiration: art, fashion, furniture, theatre, and craft products can be great and relevant sources.

183

Winson Yeung

Middleweight interior designer
Dalziel & Pow

184

Specialist in:

Retail

Title of your degree:

BA (Hons) Interior Architecture and Design

Career overview

The initial spark for my interior design passion was with Jestico + Whiles in 2012, an architectural and interior design practice with renowned expertise in education, workplace, transport, residential, and cultural facility projects around the world. After realizing Jestico + Whiles designed my secondary school and sixth form campus, I took the opportunity to do an internship at their London office where my passion for this creative profession grew. From there it drove me to study the course and pursue a career in this field.

In 2015 I accepted a placement at a company called Studio Four IV, which enabled me to see what can happen when applying your designs to real-world environments. I had the opportunity to work on various retail brands both in and outside of UK, such as Philips and Harvey Nichols. Being able to work with so many professionals in multiple fields, such as architects, creative illustrators, and graphic designers, greatly extended my knowledge and provided me with

extensive benefits in my return to my third and final year at university. It enabled me to manage and complete work before the submission date, and still gain a high grade. But, most importantly, it enabled me to help my fellow classmates with software and technical guidance, which was knowledge I gained from my experience.

Having graduated in 2017, I decided to venture out to work as a freelancer for a year. There were good and bad sides to this. The good side being the build-up of a strong foundation of your own portfolio and experience and being able to see and participate in various diverse perspectives of design. However, some projects can be short lived and work changes quickly. Nevertheless, I was able to manage projects with clients and understand more of the business side of design. I was able to see different design sectors, which exposed me to what routes I really want to pursue, and I decided that the retail branch was one of them.

I felt it was the right time to become a permanent designer and joined a new design studio, Kinnersley Kent Design, one of London and Dubai's leading architecture and interiors practices, specializing in retail, leisure, and hospitality design. I found myself placed into the in-depth technicalities of this profession, working on various scales from small to large projects, and I feel I now have a strong balance and variety of skills to offer this company due to my freelance experience. I believe joining a design company that takes on various sectors is healthy for the growth of the business and for the designers within, enabling you to explore and try other branches at one place.

$\longrightarrow$

185

Winson Yeung
portfolio excerpts

Left:
The Blonde
Hedgehog Hotel,
Winson Yeung, 2019

Left:
Harvey Nichols,
Kuwait
Four IV, 2015

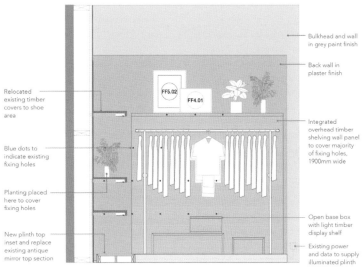

Bulkhead and wall in grey paint finish

Back wall in plaster finish

Relocated existing timber covers to shoe area

Integrated overhead timber shelving wall panel to cover majority of fixing holes, 1900mm wide

Blue dots to indicate existing fixing holes

Planting placed here to cover fixing holes

Open base box with light timber display shelf

New plinth top inset and replace existing antique mirror top section

Existing power and data to supply illuminated plinth

187

Above:
Footwear area design for
Mint Velvet, Dundrum
Kinnersley Kent Designs, 2018

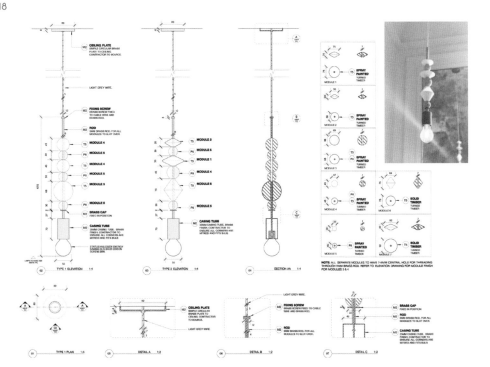

Right:
Pendant light design for
Peggy Porchsen, London
Kinnersley Kent Designs,
2019

A typical day

It varies from week to week, depending on the scale of the projects. I have been involved in all aspects of design, including concept ideation, generating visuals, material palettes, and detail drawings for both flagship and retail roll-out stores. I also help my fellow team members with their projects when required, from detail drawing packs and visuals to managing and sourcing finishes and FF&E schedules.

Working on several sites for roll-out projects has exposed me to site visits and assisting setting up planning applications for the approval process for those sites. Also, part of my role is to be responsible for material-supplier-related matters. I regularly schedule and manage meetings and liaise closely with representatives for projects.

What do you love about being an interior designer?

Every project and every client are different, meaning every challenge you face is different. The beauty of design is that we aren't just making a space look aesthetically appealing or functional for the audience, but rather understanding a vast amount of information from the industry that the project is in. For example, in retail design, when designing a jewellery store in the Middle East, a large amount of research has to be conducted first in order to venture into the actual design of the space.

The thing I love most about being a designer is reshaping the way we use space and its function. The ability to make our users think differently and hearing them say, 'I never thought it could be done or used this way' is a cherished moment to witness. I believe there is no such thing as 'normal' in design.

I believe there is no such thing as 'normal' in design.

What advice would you give to interior designers starting out in their career?

In education, finishing a design is the end of the project. In professional practices, finishing a design is only the halfway point of the project.

Architectural and interior education is different to actual experience.

When applying for a company, it doesn't matter how renowned the company is, it's what you can gain from it!

189

interior design directory

The interior design industry is tight-knit, so finding information about studios and the type of work they do can be tricky. Here you'll find the names, websites, and specialisms of over 250 UK companies to help you in your job search. As always, please consult a studio's website for the most up-to-date information.

Company	Retail	Hospitality (hotels/ bars/cafes/ restaurants)	Exhibition (events/ museums/ cultural)	Commercial (workplaces/ education/ hospitals)	Residential	Luxury transport (airplanes/ yachts/ cruiseships)	Website
1508	○	●	○	○	●	○	www.1508london.com
20.20	●	●	○	○	○	○	www.20.20.co.uk
442	●	●	○	○	○	○	www.442design.com
A-nrd	●	●	○	○	○	○	www.a-nrd.com
AD Associates	○	●	○	○	○	●	www.adassociates.london
Adeas	●	●	○	●	●	○	www.aedas.com
Afroditi Krassa	○	●	○	○	○	○	www.afroditi.com
Air Design	●	○	○	○	○	○	www.airdesign.co.uk
Alexander Waterworth Interiors	○	●	○	○	●	○	www.alexanderwaterworthinteriors.com
Alice Leigh Design	○	○	○	○	●	○	www.aliceleigh.co.uk
Align	○	○	○	●	●	○	www.aligngb.com
Allen International	●	○	○	○	○	○	www.allen-international.com
And Create	●	●	○	○	○	○	www.andcreate.co.uk
Andy Martin Architecture	●	●	○	○	●	○	www.andymartinarchitecture.com
Anita Rosato	○	●	○	○	●	○	www.anitarosato.com
Anouska Hempel Design	●	●	○	○	●	●	www.anouskahempeldesign.com
Area	○	○	○	●	○	○	www.area.co.uk
Article Design Studio	○	●	○	○	●	○	www.articledesignstudio.co.uk
Areen Design	○	●	○	●	●	●	www.areen.com
Aukett Swanke	○	●	○	●	○	○	www.aukettswanke.com
Avocado Sweets	○	●	○	○	●	○	www.avocadosweets.com
AvroKo	○	●	○	○	○	○	www.avroko.com
B3 Designers	○	●	○	●	○	○	www.b3designers.co.uk
Bailey London	○	○	○	○	●	○	www.baileylondon.com
Barber Design	●	○	○	○	○	○	www.barberdesign.co.uk
Basha-Franklin	○	○	○	●	●	○	www.basha-franklin.com
BDG	○	○	○	●	○	○	www.bdg-a-d.com
BDP	●	○	○	●	○	○	www.bdp.com
Benoy	●	●	○	○	○	○	www.benoy.com
Ben Pentreath	○	○	○	○	●	○	www.benpentreath.com
Bisset Adams	●	○	●	●	○	○	www.bissetadams.co.uk
Blacksheep	○	●	○	○	○	○	www.blacksheep.uk.com
Bluebottle	●	●	○	●	○	○	www.bluebottle.co.uk
Blueprint	○	○	○	●	○	○	www.blueprintinteriors.com
Box 9 Design	○	●	○	○	●	○	www.box-9.co.uk
Boxx Creative	○	●	○	○	○	○	www.boxx.design
Brace Studio	●	●	○	○	○	○	www.brace-studio.com
Brand Design Lab	●	○	○	○	○	○	www.branddesignlab.net
Brinkworth	●	●	●	●	●	○	www.brinkworth.com
Broadway Malyan	○	●	○	●	●	○	www.broadwaymalyan.com
Brown Studio	●	●	○	○	○	○	www.brownstudio.co.uk
Bryan O'Sullivan	○	●	○	○	●	●	www.bos-studio.com
BusbyWebb	●	●	○	○	○	○	www.busbywebb.co.uk
CADA	●	●	○	○	○	○	www.cada.co.uk
Cadmium Design	●	●	○	○	○	○	www.cadmiumdesign.co.uk
CallisonRTKL	●	●	○	○	○	○	www.callisonrtkl.com
Campbell Rigg	●	○	○	○	○	○	www.campbellrigg.com
Candy Property	○	○	○	○	●	○	www.candyandcandy.com
Cantor Masters Interior Design	○	●	○	○	●	○	www.cantormasters.com
Carey Jones Chapman Tolcher	○	●	○	●	○	○	www.cjctstudios.com
Carlisle Design Studio	○	●	○	○	●	○	www.carlisledesignstudio.com
Casson Mann	○	●	●	○	○	○	www.cassonmann.com
Catherine White Interiors	●	●	○	○	●	○	www.catherinewhiteinteriors.com
Caulder Moore	●	●	○	○	○	○	www.cauldermoore.co.uk
CC-Lab	○	○	●	○	○	○	www.cc-lab.com
Celine Estates	○	○	○	○	●	○	www.celineestates.com
Checkland Kindleysides	●	○	○	○	○	○	www.checklandkindleysides.com
Circle Square	●	○	●	○	○	○	www.circle-square.com

Company	Retail	Hospitality (hotels/ bars/cafes/ restaurants)	Exhibition (events/ museums/ cultural)	Commercial (workplaces/ education/ hospitals)	Residential	Luxury transport (airplanes/ yachts/ cruiseships)	Website
Claremont	○	○	○	●	○	○	www.claremontgi.com
CM Interior Design	●	●	○	○	○	○	www.cmdesignconsultants.com
Cocovara	○	○	○	○	●	○	www.cocovara.co.uk
Concorde BGW	○	●	○	●	○	○	www.concordebgw.com
Conran and Partners	●	●	○	●	●	○	www.conranandpartners.com
D4R	●	●	○	●	○	○	www.design4retail.co.uk
Dalziel + Pow	●	○	○	○	○	○	www.dalziel-pow.com
Darling Associates	○	●	○	●	●	○	www.darlingassociates.net
David Collins Studio	●	●	○	○	●	●	www.davidcollins.com
Daytrip	●	●	○	○	●	○	www.daytrip.studio
Denton	○	○	○	●	●	○	www.dentonassociates.com
Denton Corker Marshall	○	●	○	●	●	○	www.dentoncorkermarshall.com
Design Clarity	●	●	○	●	○	○	www.designclarity.net
Design Coalition	○	●	○	●	○	○	www.designcoalition.co.uk
Design Command	○	●	○	●	○	○	www.designcommand.co.uk
Design Haus Liberty	●	●	○	●	●	○	www.dhliberty.com
Design International	●	●	○	●	●	○	www.designinternational.com
DesignLSM	○	●	○	○	○	○	www.designlsm.com
Designmap	○	○	●	○	○	○	www.designmap.co.uk
Design Research Studio	○	●	○	●	●	●	www.designresearchstudio.net
Dexter Moren Associates	○	●	○	○	●	○	www.dextermoren.com
Dover Design	○	●	○	○	○	○	www.doverdesign.com
DTWO Design	○	●	○	○	○	○	www.dtwodesign.com
Easy Tiger	○	○	●	○	○	○	www.easytigercreative.com
Echo Architecture	●	●	○	○	○	○	www.echoarchitecture.com
EDGE	●	●	○	●	○	○	www.edgegb.com
EF Architecture & Design	○	○	○	●	○	○	www.efarchitecturedesign.com
Eight Inc	●	●	●	●	○	○	www.eightinc.com
Elicyon	○	○	○	○	●	○	www.elicyon.com
EPR Architects	○	●	○	●	●	○	www.epr.co.uk
Event	○	○	●	○	○	○	www.eventcomm.com
Fabled Studio	●	●	○	○	●	○	www.fabledstudio.com
Fabric	○	○	○	●	○	○	www.fabric.eu.com
Fenton Whelan	○	○	○	○	●	○	www.fentonwhelan.com
Fettle	○	●	○	○	○	○	www.fettle-design.co.uk
Fieldwork	●	○	○	○	○	○	www.fieldwork.co.uk
Finch Interiors	●	●	○	●	○	○	www.finchinteriors.co.uk
Fiona Barratt Interiors	○	●	○	○	●	○	www.fionabarrattinteriors.com
FITCH	●	○	●	○	○	○	www.fitch.com
Fletcher Priest Architects	○	●	○	●	○	○	www.fletcherpriest.com
Forme UK	●	●	○	●	●	○	www.forme.uk.com
FormRoom	●	●	○	●	○	○	www.formroom.com
Foster + Partners	●	●	●	●	●	●	www.fosterandpartners.com
Found Associates	●	○	○	●	●	○	www.foundassociates.com
Four By Two	●	●	○	●	○	○	www.four-by-two.com
Fourfront Group	○	○	○	●	○	○	www.fourfrontgroup.co.uk
Fran Hickman	●	●	●	●	●	○	www.franhickman.com
Fusion	○	●	○	○	○	○	www.fusiondna.co.uk
Fusion By Design	○	●	○	○	○	○	www.fusionbydesign.co.uk
Fusion Interior Group (FIG)	○	●	○	○	●	○	www.fusioninteriorsgroup.com
Futurebrand UXUS	●	●	●	●	○	○	www.futurebrand.com
G.A Group	●	●	○	○	●	○	www.thega-group.com
Gensler	●	●	●	●	○	○	www.gensler.com
George P. Johnson	○	○	●	○	○	○	www.gpj.co.uk
Glock	●	○	●	○	○	○	www.glock-uk.com
Goddard Littlefair	○	●	○	○	●	○	www.goddardlittlefair.com
gpstudio	●	●	○	○	○	○	www.gpstudio.uk.com
Grapes Design	●	●	○	○	○	○	www.grapesdesign.com

Company	Retail	Hospitality (hotels/ bars/cafes/ restaurants)	Exhibition (events/ museums/ cultural)	Commercial (workplaces/ education/ hospitals)	Residential	Luxury transport (airplanes/ yachts/ cruiseships)	Website
Green Room	●	○	○	○	○	○	www.greenroomdesign.com
Grundy + Ducker	○	●	○	○	●	○	www.gundryducker.com
GuM	○	○	●	○	○	○	www.gum.uk.com
Haley Sharpe Design (HSD)	○	○	●	○	○	○	www.haleysharpe.com
Harlequin Design	●	○	○	○	○	○	www.harlequin-design.com
Harriet Forde Design	○	●	○	○	●	○	www.hf-design.co.uk
Harrison Design	○	●	○	○	○	○	www.harrison.hn
Hassell	○	●	●	●	○	○	www.hassellstudio.com
Hawkins\Brown	○	○	○	●	○	○	www.hawkinsbrown.com
HBA	○	●	○	○	●	○	www.hba.com
Helen Green	○	○	○	○	●	○	www.helengreendesign.com
HMKM	●	○	○	○	○	○	www.hmkm.com
HOK	○	●	○	●	○	○	www.hok.com
Honest	●	●	○	○	○	○	www.thehonestbrand.com
Honky	○	○	○	○	●	○	www.honky.co.uk
Household	●	●	○	○	○	○	www.household-design.com
HPM Developments	○	○	○	○	●	●	www.hpmdevelopments.com
IA Interior Architects	●	○	○	●	○	○	www.interiorarchitects.com
I-AM	●	●	○	●	○	○	www.i-amonline.com
ID:SR	○	○	○	●	●	○	www.sheppardrobson.com
Imagination	●	●	●	○	○	○	www.imagination.com
Innovare	●	○	○	○	○	○	www.innovare-design.com
Innovision	○	○	●	○	○	○	www.weareinnovision.com
ISG	●	○	○	●	○	○	www.isgplc.com
Ivory	○	○	●	○	○	○	www.ivoryworldwide.com
JAC Group	○	○	○	●	○	○	www.jac-group.co.uk
Jackdaw Studio	○	○	○	●	○	○	www.jackdawstudio.com
Jack Morton	○	○	●	○	○	○	www.jackmorton.com
Jamie Fobert Architects	●	○	●	○	●	○	www.jamiefobertarchitects.com
Jason Bruges Studio	○	○	●	○	○	○	www.jasonbruges.com
Jestico + Whiles	○	●	●	●	●	○	www.jesticowhiles.com
JHP	●	○	○	○	○	○	www.jhp-design.com
JHR Interior design	○	○	○	○	●	○	www.jhr-interiors.com
Joyce Wang Studio	○	●	○	○	●	○	www.joycewang.com
JPA Design	○	●	○	○	○	●	www.jpadesign.com
Jump Studios	●	●	○	●	○	○	www.jump-studios.com
Kai Interiors	○	●	○	○	●	○	www.kaiinteriors.com
Katharine Pooley	○	●	○	○	●	○	www.katharinepooley.com
KCA International	○	●	○	○	●	●	www.kca-int.com
Keane	○	●	○	○	○	○	www.keanebrands.com
Kelly Hoppen	○	●	○	○	●	●	www.kellyhoppeninteriors.com
Kia Designs	○	○	○	○	●	○	www.kiadesigns.co.uk
Kinnersley Kent Design	●	●	○	○	○	○	www.kkd.co.uk
Kiwi and Pom	●	●	○	○	○	○	www.kiwiandpom.com
KONCEPT	○	●	○	○	○	○	www.konceptid.co.uk
KSS	○	●	○	●	●	○	www.kssgroup.com
Landor	●	●	●	●	○	○	www.landor.com
Lawson Robb	○	○	○	○	●	●	www.lawsonrobb.com
LOM Architecture and Design	○	○	○	●	●	○	www.lom-architecture.com
LOT	○	●	○	○	●	○	www.lot.london
Louise Bradley	○	○	○	○	●	○	www.louisebradley.co.uk
Love Interiors	○	○	○	○	●	○	www.loveinteriors.co.uk
Lumsden	●	●	●	○	○	○	www.lumsdendesign.com
Lustedgreen	●	●	○	●	●	○	www.lustedgreen.com
LXA	●	●	○	○	○	○	www.wearelxa.com
Macaulay Sinclair	○	●	○	○	○	○	www.macaulaysinclair.com
Mackenzie Wheeler	○	●	○	●	●	○	www.mackenziewheeler.co.uk
March & White	○	●	○	○	●	●	www.marchandwhite.com

Company	Retail	Hospitality (hotels/ bars/cafes/ restaurants)	Exhibition (events/ museums/ cultural)	Commercial (workplaces/ education/ hospitals)	Residential	Luxury transport (airplanes/ yachts/ cruiseships)	Website
Maris Interiors	○	○	○	●	○	○	www.maris-interiors.co.uk
Mather & Co	●	●	●	○	○	○	www.matherandco.com
Matter	○	○	●	○	○	○	www.matterxp.com
Martin Brudnizki Design Studio	○	●	○	○	●	○	www.mbds.com
Mcfarlane Latter Architects	○	●	○	●	○	○	www.mcfarlanelatter.co.uk
MCM	○	○	○	●	○	○	www.mcm-uk.com
M Design	○	○	○	●	○	○	www.mdesignlondon.com
Melt	○	●	○	○	○	○	www.meltdesignhub.com
Metaphor	○	○	●	○	○	○	www.metaphor-design.co.uk
MET Studio	○	○	●	○	○	○	www.metstudiodesign.com
Michaelis Boyd	●	●	○	○	●	○	www.michaelisboyd.com
Millington Associates	●	○	○	○	○	○	www.millingtonassociates.com
M-is	○	○	●	○	○	○	www.m-is.com
Mizzi Studio	○	●	○	●	●	○	www.mizzi.co
MKV Design	○	●	○	○	●	○	www.mkvdesign.com
M Moser Associates	○	○	○	●	○	○	www.mmoser.com
Modus	○	○	○	●	○	○	www.modus.space
Morey Smith	○	●	○	●	●	○	www.moreysmith.com
MRA	●	○	○	○	○	○	www.mra.co.uk
M Worldwide	●	○	○	○	○	○	www.mworldwide.co.uk
Mystery	○	●	○	○	○	○	www.mystery.co.uk
Nelson Design	○	●	○	○	●	○	www.nelsondesign.co.uk
Nick Leith-Smith	●	●	○	○	●	○	www.nickleithsmith.com
Nicoll Russell	●	○	○	●	●	○	www.nrsarchitects.com
No12	○	○	○	○	●	○	www.no12studio.com
Object Space Place	○	●	○	○	○	○	www.objectspaceplace.com
Oktra	○	○	○	●	○	○	www.oktra.co.uk
One Red Wall	●	○	○	○	○	○	www.oneredwall.com
Orchard	○	○	○	●	○	○	www.orchardofficedesign.co.uk
Overbury	○	●	○	●	○	○	www.overbury.com
Path	●	●	○	○	○	○	www.pathdesign.co.uk
Peldon Rose	○	○	○	●	○	○	www.peldonrose.com
Penson	○	●	○	●	○	○	www.penson.co
Perkins & Will	○	●	○	●	○	○	www.perkinswill.com
Philip Watts Design	○	●	○	○	○	○	www.philipwattsinteriors.com
Phoenix Wharf	●	●	○	○	○	○	www.phoenix-wharf.com
Plaid London	○	○	●	○	○	○	www.plaid-london.com
Portland Design	●	●	○	○	○	○	www.portland-design.com
Quinine	●	○	○	○	○	○	www.quininedesign.com
Rachel Winham	○	○	○	○	●	○	www.rachelwinham.com
Ralph Appelbaum Associates	○	○	●	○	○	○	www.raany.com
Rawls	●	○	○	○	○	○	www.rawls.co.uk
Real Studios	○	○	●	○	○	○	www.realstudios.co.uk
Red Deer	●	●	○	○	●	○	www.reddeer.co.uk
Red Frog Design	○	○	○	●	○	○	www.theredfrog.com
Redman Design	○	○	●	○	○	○	www.redman-design.co.uk
Reis Design	●	●	○	○	○	○	www.reis-design.co.uk
Residence One	○	○	○	○	●	○	www.residenceone.co.uk
Resolution Interiors	●	○	○	○	○	○	www.resolutioninteriors.com
Resonate Interiors	○	○	○	●	○	○	www.resonateinteriors.com
RDA	○	●	○	○	○	○	www.rdalimited.co.uk
Richmond International	○	●	○	○	○	○	www.richint.com
Robert Angell Design International	○	●	○	○	●	○	www.robertangelldesigninternational.com
Robert London Design	●	○	○	○	●	○	www.robertlondondesign.com
RPW Design	○	●	○	○	○	●	www.rpwdesign.co.uk
Rubicon	○	○	○	●	○	○	www.rubiconinteriors.co.uk
Run For The Hills	○	●	○	●	●	○	www.runforthehills.com
Russell Sage Studio	○	●	○	○	○	○	www.russellsagestudio.co.uk

Company	Retail	Hospitality (hotels/ bars/cafes/ restaurants)	Exhibition (events/ museums/ cultural)	Commercial (workplaces/ education/ hospitals)	Residential	Luxury transport (airplanes/ yachts/ cruiseships)	Website
RWD	○	○	○	○	○	●	www.rwd.co.uk
Sedley Place	○	●	○	○	●	○	www.sedley-place.com
Seed Design	○	●	○	○	○	○	www.seeddesign.com
Scott Brownrigg	○	●	○	●	●	○	www.scottbrownrigg.com
Shalini Misra	○	●	○	○	●	○	www.shalinimisra.com
Shaun Clarkson	○	●	○	○	●	○	www.shaunclarksonid.com
Shed	●	●	●	●	○	○	www.shed-design.com
SHH	○	●	○	○	●	○	www.shh.co.uk
Shopworks	●	○	○	○	○	○	www.shopworks.co.uk
Sibyl Colefax and John Fowler	○	○	○	○	●	○	www.sibylcolefax.com
Simple Simon Design	○	●	○	○	○	○	www.simplesimondesign.co.uk
Skyline Whitespace	○	○	●	○	○	○	www.skylinewhitespace.com
SMC Design	○	○	○	○	○	●	www.smc-design.com
Softroom	○	●	●	●	○	●	www.softroom.com
Spacelab	○	○	○	●	○	○	www.spacelab.co.uk
Spinocchia Freund	○	●	○	○	●	○	www.spinocchiafreund.com
Squire and Partners	○	●	○	●	●	○	www.squireandpartners.com
Studiofibre	●	○	○	●	○	○	www.studiofibre.com
Studio Found	●	●	○	○	○	○	www.studiofound.co.uk
Studio Indigo	○	○	○	○	●	●	www.studioindigo.co.uk
Studio MB	○	○	●	○	○	○	www.studiomb.co.uk
Studio Mica	○	●	○	○	○	○	www.studiomica.co.uk
Studio XAG	●	○	○	○	○	○	www.studioxag.com
Sybarite	●	●	○	○	○	○	www.sybarite.com
Tala Fustok	○	●	○	○	●	○	www.talafustok.co.uk
Tara Bernerd & Partners	○	●	○	○	●	●	www.tarabernerd.com
TaskSpace	○	○	○	●	○	○	www.taskspace.co.uk
Taylor Howes	○	●	○	○	●	○	www.taylorhowes.co.uk
TBA Plc	○	○	●	○	○	○	www.tbaplc.co.uk
Th2designs	○	○	○	○	●	○	www.th2designs.co.uk
The Design Solution	●	○	○	○	○	○	www.thedesignsolution.co.uk
The One Off	●	●	○	○	○	○	www.theoneoff.com
The Yard Creative	●	●	○	○	○	○	www.theyardcreative.com
Thirdway Interiors	○	○	○	●	○	○	www.thirdwayinteriors.com
Tibbatts Abel	○	●	○	○	○	○	www.tibbattsabel.com
Tonik Associates	●	●	○	○	○	○	www.tonikassociates.co.uk
TP Bennett	○	●	○	●	○	○	www.tpbennett.com
Trevillion Interiors	○	●	○	●	○	○	www.trevillion.co.uk
Turnerbates	○	●	○	●	○	○	www.turnerbates.com
Twelve	●	●	○	○	○	○	www.twelve-studio.co.uk
Unispace	○	○	○	●	○	○	www.unispace.com
United Design Partnership	○	●	○	○	●	○	www.united-designpartnership.com
Universal Design Studio	●	●	●	●	○	○	www.universaldesignstudio.com
Virgile + Partners	●	●	○	○	○	○	www.virgileandpartners.com
Volume Creative	●	●	○	○	○	●	www.volumecreative.co.uk
Wanda Creative	●	○	○	○	○	○	www.wanda.uk.com
WATG	○	●	○	○	○	○	www.watg.com
WISH London	○	●	○	●	●	○	www.wish-london.co.uk
Wonder	○	○	●	○	○	○	www.wonderlondon.com
Wood Design and Management	○	○	●	○	○	○	www.woodint.co.uk
Woods Bagot	●	●	○	●	●	○	www.woodsbagot.com
Workplace Creations	○	○	○	●	○	○	www.workplace-creations.co.uk
Yoo	○	●	○	○	●	○	www.yoo.com
YourStudio	●	●	●	○	○	○	www.weareyourstudio.com
Zaha Hadid Architects	●	○	●	○	●	○	www.zaha-hadid.com
Zebra	●	●	○	○	○	○	www.zbr.co.uk

Author: Lucy Painter, Studio *www.studio.eu.com*

Design and art direction: Ark *www.designbyark.co.uk*

Portrait photography: Theo McInnes *www.theomcinnes.com*

Illustration: Beth Goody *www.bethgoody.com*

First edition printed in the United Kingdom,
January 2020 on FSC certified uncoated paper.